**NEW DIRECTIONS
FOR EXCEPTIONAL
CHILDREN**

Number 2 • 1980

NEW DIRECTIONS
FOR EXCEPTIONAL
CHILDREN

A Quarterly Sourcebook
James J. Gallagher, Editor-in-Chief

Number 2, 1980

Language Intervention
with Children

Diane Bricker
Guest Editor

Jossey-Bass Inc., Publishers
San Francisco • Washington • London

LANGUAGE INTERVENTION WITH CHILDREN
New Directions for Exceptional Children
Number 2, 1980
        Diane Bricker, Guest Editor

New Directions for Exceptional Children is published
quarterly by Jossey-Bass Inc., Publishers. Subscriptions are
available at the regular rate for institutions, libraries, and
agencies of $30 for one year. Individuals may subscribe at the
special professional rate of $18 for one year.

Correspondence:
Subscriptions, single-issue orders, change of address notices,
undelivered copies, and other correspondence should be sent to
New Directions Subscriptions, Jossey-Bass Inc., Publishers,
433 California Street, San Francisco, California 94104.
Editorial correspondence should be sent to the Editor-in-Chief,
James J. Gallagher, Graham Child Development Center,
University of North Carolina, Chapel Hill,
North Carolina 27514.

Library of Congress Catalogue Card Number LC 79-92039

Cover design by Willi Baum
Manufactured in the United States of America

Contents

vi

Editor's Notes

The growth in the understanding of communicative processes and their effect on related language intervention approaches has produced significant changes in the field and expansions in our knowledge base during the past decade. Unfortunately, the transmission of research-based innovations to the practitioner's level is a lengthy process. Thus, a major hurdle facing interventionists is access to, in a reasonable time frame, more effective methods, and content for language intervention. In effect the problem seems to be the translation and flow of information. The purpose of this volume is to provide the teacher, clinician, and other on-line interventionists with such a translation. A practical synthesis of the more useful and exciting new approaches to language intervention is offered with the hope that the reader integrates this information into both his conceptual framework and behavioral repertoire.

The contributors to this volume recognize that the interventionist's time is largely occupied by attempting to manage the ongoing daily needs of children having a variety of communication disorders. Often little time remains for searching through the literature for solutions to complex problems. In this volume the individual contributors have already done much of the necessary sorting of available literature and research and have extracted important information for practitioners to consider for inclusion into their programs. The emphasis is on the discussion of general principles or approaches that can be usefully applied in intervention settings:

Communication problems seen in children vary considerably from mild delays to the total absence of language. Effective intervention with a continuum of language disorders requires a number of different approaches or strategies; therefore, this volume contains descriptions of intervention strategies useful with the handicapped infant, the hearing impaired child, the nonspeech child, and the mildly language delayed child. A foundation for the discussion of intervention strategies for specific populations of language delayed children is needed to provide a historical perspective which links the past to our contemporary views of language development and intervention. Further, it seems essential to provide the reader with a broadly based ecological model from which to view the child, his family and the objectives of language intervention.

In each chapter the emphasis is on helping the practitioner understand the function of communication for the child. Without this understanding, programs will continue to put children through sterile routines that have little to do with the acquisition and use of a generative language system.

Diane Bricker
Guest Editor

Diane Bricker is currently a professor of special education and director of the Preschool Program, Center on Human Development, University of Oregon. Her professional career has focused on two major areas of interest: the development of effective intervention programs for young handicapped children and the development of language programs with an emphasis on broadly based communicative functions.

*Understanding the history of language intervention provides
the reader with a useful foundation from which to view
contemporary trends. Those trends having major influence
on current directions in language intervention are described
and their future evolution predicted.*

Synthesis of Trends in Language Intervention

Richard L. Schiefelbusch

In 1959 at a public disclosure about the newly begun Parsons Project, I made
the observation that whereas speech specialists have generally discouraged the
prospect of speech therapy with mentally retarded children, the same children
had reciprocated by rejecting the methods employed by speech specialists.
That this mutual rejection was acknowledged at this time by a polite chuckle
is, I have decided, rather surprising since the topic is essentially not humorous.

Experience suggests that the feasibility of an instructional undertaking
depends upon a mutual acquaintance of the participants and upon a sense of
shared reality. If the instructors have little confidence or competence to bring
to the task—if their designs are incomplete or tenuous—the learner may
indeed seem to be unpromising. The end result of the circular thinking that
was prevalent then led to the assumption that a considerable range of the communicatively handicapped were not suitable learners, hence the terms *subtrainable* and *unteachable*.

Perhaps, however, the acceptance-rejection issue was a distortion of
the real issue. Stevenson (1962, p.4) suggested that "the study of the language
of the handicapped has not (up to now) been an attractive field into which to
recruit research persons. Persons interested in basic research have sought their
subjects from other groups. Little progress can be expected until research per-

sons interested in basic research do enter the field in greater numbers." This analysis seems to be an aspersion against the small group of professionals who attempted to teach speech and language to severely impaired individuals prior to 1962. The statement also reveals Stevenson's preoccupation with basic as compared to applied or clinical research; however, I regard his analysis as essentially correct. Subsequent events have emphasized the accuracy of this position better than Stevenson could have predicted from the meager information available at the time. It is apparent now that an increasing number of scientists have contributed enormously to the feasibility of speech, language and communication intervention during the past fifteen to twenty years. The infusion of basic and applied researchers was the exciting force that established the field of language intervention as an acceptable scientific endeavor. The analysis of this development comprises the main effort of this chapter, and hopefully will permit the synthesis of trends that is promised in the title.

Trends

A trend is a tendency that we talk about a great deal, but seldom bother to verify. Yet in the absence of such direct verification, observers agree that indeed there are trends in language intervention. For the most part this writer has attempted to identify the writings which highlight the trends. As I do this I shall occasionally hide behind historical license; but, for the most part, I shall use forthright reporting.

We now have enough varied experiences, applied research, and cherished opinions that we can productively discuss trends. Hopefully such considerations will not increase the disagreements or the dissonance, but will make us more evaluative, more insightful and more aware of our current status.

These trends can be viewed in a positive manner because we are becoming mature and honest in our informal discourse about language teaching while, at the same time, we have more solid information to talk about and more experience to share. Nevertheless, it may be a little early in our progress to synthesize trends. But then, pehaps we can all agree on a slight alteration of the time-honored cliche: Better early than never.

Historical Overview

In his comprehensive chapter on "Language and Communication of Mental Defectives," Spradlin (1963a) pointed out that prior to that time, most of the field's attention had been on speech behavior. Spreen (1965) subsequently did a systematic job of examining the incidence figures bearing on speech performance. He found, not surprisingly, that the highest incidence figures were for children with the lowest intelligence and that incidence figures dropped as the intelligence level increased. A number of incidence studies of institutionalized children conducted between 1950 and 1957 revealed figures varying between two thirds and three fourths of these populations having speech or language disorders. Other studies that examined types of errors were summarized by Mathews (1957) with the statement, "There is no evidence to suggest that the speech defects of the mentally retarded differ in kind from those of a nonretarded, speech-defective population."

This focal issue of quantitative differences may have served as a deterrent to clinical intervention programs: planners simply estimated the progress the retarded and other severely disabled individuals were likely to make in clinical programs and concluded that other categories of clients could progress faster. If a criterion of progress were used as the basis of selection, obviously the seriously impaired individual would rate a low priority. The full implications relating to these impaired individuals were apparently not considered when excluding them from the programs of language and communication intervention. There were few systematic speech and hearing intervention studies reported prior to 1960.

Nineteen-fifty seven was a vintage year for the development of a practical field of child language. Osgood (1957) published, "A Behavioristic Analysis of Perception and Language as Cognitive Phenomena," in which he described a behavioral approach for dealing with the complex aspects of language. This psycholinguistic system was used by Sievers and Essa (1961) to develop the Differential Language Facility Test (DLFT). Kirk and McCarthy (1961) used this work as a springboard for the development of the Illinois Test of Psycholinguistic Abilities (ITPA). The widespread use of the ITPA is reason enough to consider Osgood's formulations to be an important contribution to language teaching in the educational domain. The work is especially prominent in the field of learning disabilities. Recently Hollis and Schiefelbusch (1979) have used Osgood's model as a basic system for analyzing the nonspeech language approaches used with severely retarded, autistic, and cerebral palsied children.

The year 1957 also saw the publication of Skinner's *Verbal Behavior*. The behavioral analyses contained in this book were used by Spradlin (1963b) to develop the Parsons Language Sample (PLS). Spradlin did not attempt to standardize his test, preferring instead to emphasize experimental work on interpersonal variables and contingency management of language behavior. Neither the ITPA nor the PLS incorporated a generative linguistic model of language. Although Chomsky's *Syntactic Structures* was also published in 1957, his theory of transformational grammar did not have an impact on language evaluations of the more seriously language disordered for several years. Carroll (1967) was one of the first to point out the intriguing possibilities of a transformational grammar for this population, similar to that used in studying language acquisition of normal preschool children.

It is ironic that major contributions to language intervention should have been made by systems which, on the surface, appear to be theoretically incompatible. I refer, of course, to *generative grammar* (Chomsky) and *operant conditioning* (Skinner). The latter made an impact upon the field after formulations were designed in basic laboratories, notably at Harvard and Columbia, and in a few applied settings such as Parsons State Hospital, Ranier School, Anna State Hospital, and Metropolitan Hospital. The work at Parsons combined the functions of interpersonal language with behavioral designs. The Parsons group was especially influenced by Skinner's *Verbal Behavior* (1957). The results from these laboratory investigations and subsequent programs were to enhance effective implementation, management, and evaluation systems for language intervention work. The spectacular outcome was the designing of functional language and communication programs for moderately and severely handicapped children. A range of new learners was added to the training scene. In the period from 1958 to 1970 a new field of functional training activity was born. It was controversial and overly optimistic, but the impact of the early behavior modifiers was to create a field of clinical behavior management and to bring increasing numbers of speech, language, and communication programs into educational settings. In particular, I refer to the work on antecedent and subsequent events; on sustained attention; on increased or decreased rates of responding; and on imitation and auditory test functions. This and related behavioral work established the basis for clinical management for a large number of individuals with limited language. A behavioral technology for initiating and maintaining language training with difficult-to-manage persons became a practical reality for virtually all handicapped individuals.

Nevertheless, critical evaluators of these activities during subsequent years raised serious questions about the lack of a complete language system— especially about the failure of the behaviorists to adopt the generative designs that the psycholinguists were employing to conduct research with young children. Consequently, in the period from 1965 to 1970 critical voices swelled into a loud clamor. Interestingly, a number of clinicians and intervention research specialists began as early as 1965 to probe for generative effects and otherwise to use the data on language acquisition to plan developmental language systems that could be taught in behaviorally oriented language programs—in particular the work of Guess, Sailor, Baer, and Sherman at the Kansas Neurological Institute (Baer and Guess, 1971; Schumaker and Sherman, 1970). By 1970 one could hardly find a comprehensive language program for the severely handicapped that did not employ both systems in some fashion. In effect the explicit events of a generative language system became the behavioral events recorded on cumulative records, the criterion measures, and the probe measures of the behaviorists. Substantial evidence of the synthesis of these systems is presented in McLean, Yoder, and Schiefelbusch (1972), in Schiefelbusch and Lloyd (1974), and in Schiefelbusch (1978a, b).

A second major synthesis, also remarkably apparent in current publications, can trace its beginnings back to about 1970. I refer to the emergence of semantic frames of reference and the close relationship between the acquisition of semantic functions and the emergence of cognitive stages of development. (For a historic analysis of the blending of cognitive and behavioral functions see Staats (1974) and for the combining of developmental psycholinguistics and cognitive issues see Section II in Schiefelbusch and Lloyd, 1974.)

The emergence of cognitive designs in early intervention programs and the utilization of cognitive-semantic planning has opened up strikingly interesting and productive programs for training any child who is in the early phases of language acquisition. The origin of this work goes back to Piaget's early work (for instance, *The Language and Thought of the Child,* 1926). The validity of the statement by Bowerman (1974, p. 192) that the "recent" interest in the cognitive underpinnings of language can be attributed to the "discovery" of Piaget by developmental psycholinguists who are increasingly appreciating the implications of his work for a theory of language development is apparent. Prominent among other cognitively oriented investigators are Ol'eron (1977), Morehead and Morehead (1976), and Bowerman (1978). Leonard (1978) recently examined cognitive stages in light of remedial language designs and has summarized much of the earlier work in this area.

Just as language emerged as a major development in intervention research in the sixties, communication has emerged in the seventies. A prominent area of communication research is pragmatics (the study of language use). A widely cited definition of pragmatics is that of Charles Morris (1946) who divides linguistic science into three areas: (1) syntactics—the relations holding among signs; (2) semantics—the relations between signs and their referents; (3) pragmatics—the relations between signs and their human users.

However, Bates (1976) points out that pragmatics should not be considered as another kind of sign relation equivalent to syntactics and semantics. It should rather be considered as the interface between linguistic, cognitive, and social development. This position permits the bridging of psycholinguistic theory and general developmental research.

Rees (1978) has related pragmatic theory and a number of applied issues to normal and disordered language development and concludes that, "The possibilities, . . . for effective application of the pragmatic approach to studying and remediating clinical populations seem almost limitless. Without doubt the future will bring a wealth of studies and reports on this subject that will advance clinical knowledge and skills for training the use of language in context" (p. 263).

One could conclude from the history section that the past twenty years has taken us from initial distinct theories to integrated applications and from a condition of apathy and confusion to fully developed language intervention programs. However, such a conclusion is an oversimplification which excludes a number of potent functional areas. I shall mention a few such areas and explain briefly why their omission would be a serious blunder.

Contemporary Analysis

The historical overview section was designed to examine the contributions of important theories and applications of these theories, but it did not explain how the identified functional developments have been synthesized into intervention models and strategies. An advantage of moving the current synthesizing effort into the instructional domain is that we can better consider the feasibility of designs. This enables us, in part at least, to avoid "The Language Game" discussed by Bricker and Bricker (1974). The language game as they identify it involves the bias and selectivity based on theoretical preoccupations that often leads to an adversary relationship between professionals with disparate views.

Having spent time in the previous section identifying theoretical contributions and suggesting their applications to language training, either singly or in combination, I am not intending to denigrate theoretical approaches. However, I should like to make the point that applications have been and seem to be increasingly functional. There is an identifiable procedure in this programming. It may be described simply as a rational effort to design the best program of instruction that the specialist can fashion and then to refine it and improve it through instructional experience. There is an increasing purposefulness about both the designing and the refining.

Examples of designed and refined programs are presented by Miller and Yoder (1974), Guess, Sailor, and Baer (1974), Ruder and Smith (1974), Bricker, Ruder, and Vincent (1976), Hollis and Carrier (1978), and Waryas and Stremel-Campbell (1978). Bases for planning and developing language intervention programs have been discussed by Miller (1978), Ruder (1978), and Guess, Keogh, and Sailor (1978). Schiefelbusch (1978b) suggests that efforts to examine such programs requires the consideration of strategies. Strategies can be grouped into four classes: general strategies, design strategies, instructional strategies, and program strategies.

The increasing attention to intervention strategies, decision making, and instructional planning suggests that intervention research is becoming more apt in considering the complex issues in language training. This sophistication is apparent in planning language simulation programs for infants and preschool children (Bricker and Bricker, 1974; Bricker, Ruder, and Vincent, 1976; Bruner, 1977; Fowler, forthcoming; Ramey, Sparling, and Wasik, forthcoming). Also, designs have been developed for nonspeech communication board programs for cerebral palsied children (Harris and Vanderheiden, 1979; McNaughton, 1979). Sign programs have been designed for autistic children (Alpert, 1979; Creedon, 1973; McLean and McLean, 1974; Schaeffer, 1979). Visually oriented programs have also been developed for severely retarded children (Wollman, 1979; Carrier, 1979; Hodges and Deich, 1979) and multiply handicapped children (Hollis and Carrier, 1978; Wulz and Hollis, 1979). Functional programs have been designed for severely impaired children (Guess, Sailor, and Baer, 1978; Waryas and Stremel-Campbell, 1978). Additionally, designers have prepared programs for parents (Schumaker and Sherman, 1978).

An important fact about each of these carefully designed programs is that they could not have been developed fifteen years ago. This assertion highlights the impact of current design technology and current psycholinguistic knowledge and suggests that current language research is moving rapidly toward the development of more effective language and communication programs. However, important as these developments may be we should not assume that the essential means for teaching functional language to the handicapped has been accomplished. There are a number of important issues that need further research and still others for which major conceptualization or models are required before objectives can be achieved.

Projected Trends

There have been several general trends in child language activities in recent years. One trend is denoted by the term *child-language*. The term designates an area in which child development specialists, speech and hearing specialists, special teachers, psycholinguists, cognitive and experimental psychologists, cultural anthropologists, and other language specialists can converge and join efforts. This natural conflux of research activity is almost certain to produce new patterns of study and new intervention designs. We seem at last to have comprehended the instrumentality of language in the lives of children. As a consequence we have begun to track the language acquisition patterns of children beginning with the birth cry and extending to the development of adult roles. This enormous undertaking is predicated on an interdisciplinary effort without which the task could not be accomplished.

The interdisciplinary effort will continue to provide comprehensive models and theories guiding the efforts of specialists with diverse interests. The research on both language acquisition and intervention will be greatly influenced by the composite undertaking. The impact on intervention has already begun as illustrated by the work of Schiefelbusch and Lloyd (1974), Muma (1978), Bloom and Lahey (1978), and Schiefelbusch (1978a, b).

Eventual developments within the child-language field are hard to predict, but basic trends can be foreseen. For instance, the trend toward a further synthesis of areas will continue. This synthesis will likely focus sharply on developmental functions and will combine cognitive and linguistic systems with an evolving instructional science. Also prominent in this effort will be rapidly improving tactics for denoting the critical individual plan. Thus, the effectiveness of teaching language to impaired children, deprived children, abused children, retarded children, and inscrutable children will be improved. Clinical research efforts will likely produce a major portion of the important data that shapes and guides future work. This facilitation effort seems to draw heavily upon the biomedical and the socioeducational fields, but also is integrally associated with the behavioral, cognitive, and linguistic sciences. A second general trend is denoted by the term *social competence* and by the less comprehensive term *pragmatic functions*. The first requirement signaled by this trend is that language should be functional. Teaching functional language systems requires knowledge of the ways infants and small children socialize, process information, learn skills, perceive the world, and seek affection. It also seems likely that functional language acquisition closely parallels the acquisition of conceptual and other cognitive information. Further, researchers have observed that the social transactions of infants and small children provide much of the context for early language learning. This is an area of intensive investigation and should generate increasingly useful information.

The early acquisition periods are keyed to affectional exchanges, and to intonational and protoaction (for instance, peek-a-boo) games. The establishment of effective communication transactions in early social experience appears to lead to other language competencies in succeeding months. We are likely to want to know how this process occurs and how to facilitate the child's movement to formal language.

Also we are likely to seek information on how symbol systems serve the development of cognitive and social competence. The degree to which practice — the amount of talking and listening a child experiences — affects the development of linguistic competence is also likely to be a prominent issue in subsequent research. Cromer's (forthcoming) epigenetic formulation may assist in the determination of acquisitional influences that derive from both genetic and environmental influences. At stake in this research effort is the development of a theory of language acquisition. Also at stake may be the future investments that are made in infant and preschool stimulation and other early language programs.

Pragmatics, as a subarea of linguistics, centers on the study of language. as a social system with rules for correct performance in given social, situational and linguistic contexts. Individuals who generally observe these rules of discourse are judged to be communicatively competent. The competent speaker adjusts his message to take into account many extralinguistic contextual factors, such as the comparative status of one's listener, the type of social situation in which one is engaged, and the inferred knowledge and beliefs of the listener.

Current interest in pragmatics has been spurred by the work of a number of specialists. The work of Bates (1976) interrelates cognitive and social behavior while Rees (1978) has extended the theory of pragmatic competence to clinical strategies. Other work will follow shortly. Probably the issue of pragmatics will soon draw as much attention as have the syntactic and semantic features of language. Three special developments in the pragmatics literature should be especially useful to language interventionists. These are: (1) a taxonomy of pragmatic functioning, (2) delineations about the acquisition of communicative competence, and (3) strategies for teaching pragmatic functions.

A third general trend involves language interventions for infants and small children. A number of studies of early perception (Butterfield and Cairns, 1974; Eimas, 1974; Trehub, Bull, and Schneider, forthcoming), mother-infant interaction (Thoman, 1978; Ainsworth and Bell, 1974), and prelinguistic language and communication (Sugarman-Bell, 1978) have stamped infancy as a critical period for the development of competence. Interventions usually are designed for infants "at-risk" for the acquisition of language functions; that is, those in danger of being derailed from the normal track of acquiring skill in language use. Early detection of risk conditions may specify developmental problems or gross inadequacies in the environment of the infant. The less intransigent conditions may be erased by appropriate daily stimulation and care. Intensive efforts are now underway to specify the parameters of early detection and intervention (Minifie and Lloyd, 1978; Osofsky, 1979; Tjossem, 1976).

The current state of knowledge in this area suggests that stimulating environments can be specified (Bricker, Seibert, and Casuso, 1980) and that parent instruction can lead to important improvements in language and communication functions (Beller, 1979; Horton, 1974). At this stage of infant research it is clear that early intervention is feasible. Detection and intervention designs have been verified. Future studies, however, must carefully specify the gains that can be expected under a range of possible conditions. Also, the issue of long term effects and the generalization of functions must be investigated. There is a strong surge of interest in the welfare of infants and small children during 1979, the International Year of the Child. However, it may be too early to predict the strength of this interest. Issues that are certain to receive increasing attention are sociocultural retardation (Ramey and Mills, 1975), early intervention for the severely handicapped (Bricker, Seibert, and Casuso, 1980), and early intervention for augmentative language programs (McDonald, 1979; Shane, 1979).

A fourth general trend is toward alternative modes of language designed to fit the individual differences of children with severely limited capabilities for speech (Harris and Vanderheiden, 1979; Moores, 1974; Shane, 1979). The issues for this development stem in part from research with the great apes (Fouts, Couch, and O'Neil, 1979; Premack, 1970; Rumbaugh, 1977). However, more directly it derives from extensive experience with sign language, communication boards, language transactions involving plastic tokens, and electronically presented symbol systems. It is speculated (Schiefelbusch and Hollis, 1979) that nonspeech strategies will receive increasing attention in the language programs for severely impaired children. The disability categories most frequently mentioned are deaf, autistic, cerebral palsied, and retarded children. However, it should be mentioned that multiply handicapped children often have the greatest deficit in language acquisition and have the greatest need for alternative systems (Hollis and Carrier, 1978).

Emphasis on nonspeech language programs seems to signal a shift from speaking as a terminal objective to language usage. We seem now to understand that a child at any age needs to have a symbol system with which to transact and perhaps to control his environment. Further, the child needs to have effective communication tools at an early age so that they can serve as a bases for cognitive learning and social interaction. We must assume the position that communicative skills may be acquired with whatever modality and channel available to the child in receptive and expressive processing.

A fifth general trend is ecological in nature. Intervention specialists have become increasingly aware that the child uses language differently in various environmental contexts. The language skills that are trained may not generalize to contexts in the child's natural environment (Rogers-Warren and Warren, 1977). The taught language may not prove to be functional in meeting the child's needs in settings beyond the training environment. In the ecological designs for language intervention, parents are receiving more and more attention (Schumaker and Sherman, 1978). For instance, training parents to work with infants and small children, especially those that are autistic, deaf, and motorically disabled is the primary strategy selected for teaching them functional language.

The emphasis upon ecological issues and upon parents in particular reflects the increasing knowledge about how language is learned, used, and altered. The impact of environmental planning and designing is sure to be increasingly apparent in the years to come (Hart and Rogers-Warren, 1978).

Finally, there is a discernable trend toward combining cognitive and behavioral approaches to language learning. Staats (1974) provided a detailed, critical analysis of the schism that developed between behavioral and cognitive systems during the 50s and 60s. Even during the early 70s, it was assumed that the theoretical views of Skinner and Chomsky could not be integrated. At Chula Vista Lodge in Wisconsin, a major step in combining the theories of Skinner, Chomsky, and Piaget was taken in 1973. The result of this intertheoretical conference was the book, *Language Perspectives—Acquisition, Retardation, and Intervention*. The primary message of the conference and the book was that behavioral and cognitive systems can be combined and should of necessity be combined to form viable systems of language intervention. The book also reported on experimental programs of language training in which linguistic and behavioral systems had already been combined.

During the past six years there has been an increasing demonstration that cognitive and behavioral systems are compatible (Mahoney, 1974; Meichenbaum, 1977). However, the most impressive evidence emerges from systems of taught language. The competence of current designs are certain to be improved as we gain a better grasp of the language functions to be taught and as we understand better how to design functional environments in which to teach them.

The general trends just described certainly do not exhaust the list of potential future developments. For instance, the issue of individualization is due to receive increasing attention. We have learned to use assessment as an important feature of intervention (Miller, 1978) and to consider the functional abilities of severely impaired children (Shane, 1979). We also are attempting to teach a wider range of children in mainstream circumstances. Consequently, we shall be forced more and more to design functional programs that are adaptive to the individualized needs and aptitudes of each child.

Another future trend will be observed in the range and variety of valid data systems that are employed. The complex nature of language and communication phenomena will require more sensitive designs for perceiving, handling, and analyzing data. A further complexity is the variety of contexts, including natural contexts, in which we seek to record functional interactions.

Still another trend to expect is better language curricula and better programming. This development will reflect improved basic information about language as a system and about how that system is learned and employed. The functional nature of that system must be considered in teaching it. The emphasis will be on teaching a functional language designed to serve the particular needs and arrangements of the person to whom it is taught.

The reader can undoubtedly think of other likely trends. Together we can agree that the most likely trend of all is that language research and clinical experience will create better approaches, better methods, and better programs. These developments, in turn, will lead to more effective intervention plans for handicapped children.

References

Ainsworth, M. D. S., and Bell, J. M. "Mother-Infant Interaction and the Development of Competence." In K. Connolly and J. Bruner (Eds.), *The Growth of Competence.* New York: Academic Press, 1974.

Alpert, C. "Vocal and Nonvocal Aspects of Communication in the Autistic Child." In R. L. Schiefelbusch (Ed.), *Nonspeech Language and Communication.* Baltimore: University Park Press, 1979.

Baer, D. M., and Guess, D. "Receptive Training of Adjectival Inflections in Mental Retardates." *Journal of Applied Behavior Analysis, 1971, 4,* 129–141.

Bates, E. *Language and Context: The Acquisition of Pragmatics.* New York: Academic, 1976.

Beller, E. "Early Intervention Programs." In J. D. Osofsky (Ed.), *Handbook of Infant Development.* New York: Wiley 1979.

Bloom, L., and Lahey, M. *Language Development and Language Disorders.* New York: Wiley, 1978.

Bowerman, M. "Development of Concepts Underlying Language." In R. L. Schiefelbusch and L. L. Lloyd (Eds.), *Language Perspectives: Acquisition, Retardation, and Intervention.* Baltimore: University Park Press, 1974.

Bowerman, M. "Semantic and Syntactic Development: A Review of What, When, and How in Language Intervention." Baltimore: University Park Press, 1978.

Bricker, D. D., Ruder, K. F., and Vincent, L. "An Intervention Strategy for Language Deficient Children." In N. G. Haring and R. L. Schiefelbusch (Eds.), *Teaching Special Children*. New York: McGraw-Hill, 1976.

Bricker, D. D., Seibert, J. M., and Casuso, V. "Early Intervention." In J. Hogg and P. Mittler (Eds.), *Advances in Mental Handicap Research*. New York: Wiley, 1980.

Bricker, W. A., and Bricker, D. D. "An Early Language Training Strategy." In R. L. Schiefelbusch and L. L. Lloyd (Eds.), *Language Perspectives: Acquisition, Retardation, Intervention*. Baltimore: University Park Press, 1974.

Bruner, J. S. "Early Social Interaction and Language Acquisition." In H. R. Schaffer (Ed.), *Studies in Mother-Infant Interaction*. New York: Academic Press, 1977.

Butterfield, E. C., and Cairns, G. F. "Infant Reception Research." In R. L. Schiefelbusch and L. L. Lloyd (Eds.), *Language Perspectives: Acquisition, Retardation, and Intervention*. Baltimore: University Park Press, 1974.

Carrier, J. K. "Application of Functional Analysis and a Nonspeech Response Mode to Teaching Language." In R. L. Schiefelbusch and J. H. Hollis (Eds.), *Language Intervention from Ape to Child*. Baltimore: University Park Press, 1979.

Carroll, J. B. "Psycholinguists in the Study of Mental Retardation." In R. L. Schiefelbusch, R. H. Copeland, and J. O. Smith (Eds.), *Language and Mental Retardation*. New York: Holt, Rinehart, and Winston, 1967.

Chomsky, N. *Syntactic Structures*. The Hague, Netherlands: Mouton, 1957.

Creedon, M. P. (Ed.). *Appropriate Behavior Through Communication: A New Program in Simultaneous Language*. Chicago: Dysfunctioning Child Center, Michael Reese Medical Center, 1973.

Cromer, R. F. "Reconceptualizing Language Acquisition and Language Development." In R. L. Schiefelbusch and D. D. Bricker (Eds.), *Early Language Intervention*. Baltimore: University Park Press, forthcoming.

Eimas, P. D. "Linguistic Processing of Speech by Young Infants." In R. L. Schiefelbusch and L. L. Lloyd (Eds.), *Language Perspectives: Acquisition, Retardation, and Intervention*. Baltimore: University Park Press, 1974.

Fouts, R. S., Couch, J. B., and O'Neil, C. R. "Strategies for Primate Language Training." In R. L. Schiefelbusch and J. H. Hollis (Eds.), *Language Intervention from Ape to Child*. Baltimore: University Park Press, 1979.

Fowler, W. "A Strategy for Infant Learning and Developmental Learning." In R. L. Schiefelbusch and D. D. Bricker (Eds.), *Early Language Intervention*. Baltimore: University Park Press, forthcoming.

Guess, D., Keogh, W., and Sailor, W. "Generalization of Speech and Language Behavior: Measurement and Training Tactics." In R. L. Schiefelbusch (Ed.), *Bases of Language Intervention*. Baltimore: University Park Press, 1978.

Guess, D., Sailor, W., and Baer, D. M. "To Teach Language to Retarded Children." In R. L. Schiefelbusch and L. L. Lloyd (Eds.), *Language Perspectives: Acquisition, Retardation and Intervention*. Baltimore: University Park Press, 1974.

Guess, D., Sailor, W., and Baer, D. M. "Children with Limited Language." In R. L. Schiefelbusch (Ed.), *Language Intervention Strategies*. Baltimore: University Park Press. 1978.

Harris, D., and Vanderheiden, G. "Augmentative Communication Techniques for Nonvocal Severely Physically Handicapped Children." In R. L. Schiefelbusch (Ed.), *Nonspeech Language and Communication*. Baltimore: University Park Press, 1979.

Hart, B., and Rogers-Warren, A. "A Milieu Approach to Teaching Language." In R. L. Schiefelbusch (Ed.), *Language Intervention Strategies*. Baltimore: University Park Press, 1978.

Hodges, P., and Deich, R. F. "Language Intervention Strategies with Manipulable Symbols." In R. L. Schiefelbusch and J. H. Hollis (Eds.), *Language Intervention Strategies*. Baltimore: University Park Press, 1979.

Hollis, J. H., and Carrier, J. K. "Intervention Strategies for Nonspeech Children." In R. L. Schiefelbusch (Ed.), *Language Intervention Strategies*. Baltimore: University Park Press, 1978.

Hollis, J. H., and Schiefelbusch, R. L. "A General System for Language Analysis." In R. L. Schiefelbusch and J. H. Hollis (Eds.), *Language Intervention from Ape to Child*. Baltimore: University Park Press, 1979.

Horton, K. B. "Infant Intervention and Language Learning." In R. L. Schiefelbusch and L. L. Lloyd (Eds.), *Language Perspectives: Acquisition, Retardation, and Intervention*. Baltimore: University Park Press, 1974.

Kirk, S. A., and McCarthy, J. J. "Illinois Test of Psycholinguistic Abilities—An Approach to Differential Diagnosis." *American Journal of Mental Deficiency*, 1961, *66*, 399–412.

Leonard, L. B. "Cognitive Factors in Early Linguistic Development." In R. L. Schiefelbusch (Ed.), *Bases of Language Intervention*. Baltimore: University Park Press, 1978.

McDonald, E. T. "Children at Risk in the Development of Intelligible Speech." In R. L. Schiefelbusch (Ed.), *Nonspeech Language and Communication*. Baltimore: University Park Press, 1979.

McLean, J. E., Yoder, D. E., and Schiefelbusch, R. L. (Eds.), *Language Intervention with the Retarded*. Baltimore: University Park Press, 1972.

McLean, L. P., and McLean, J. E. "A Language Training Program for Nonverbal Autistic Children." Journal of Speech and Hearing Disorders, 1974, *39*, 186–193.

McNaughton, S. "The Application of Blissymbolics." In R. L. Schiefelbusch (Ed.), *Nonspeech Language and Communication*. Baltimore: University Park Press, 1979.

Mahoney, M. J. *Cognition and Behavior Modification*. Cambridge, Mass.: Ballinger, 1974.

Mathews, J. "Speech Problems of the Mentally Retarded." In L. E. Travis (Ed.), *Handbook of Speech Pathology*. New York: Appleton-Century-Crofts, 1957.

Meichenbaum, D. *Cognitive Behavior Modification*. New York: Plenum Press, 1977.

Miller, J. F. "Assessing Children's Language Behavior." In R. L. Schiefelbusch (Ed.), *Bases of Language Intervention*. Baltimore: University Park Press, 1978.

Miller, J. F., and Yoder, D. E. "An Ontogenetic Language Teaching Strategy for Retarded Children." In R. L. Schiefelbusch and L. L. Lloyd (Eds.), *Language Perspectives: Acquisition, Retardation, and Intervention*. Baltimore: University Park Press, 1974.

Minifie, F. D., and Lloyd, L. L. (Eds.), *Communicative and Cognitive Abilities—Early Behavior Assessment*. Baltimore: University Park Press, 1978.

Moores, D. F. "Nonvocal Systems of Verbal Behavior." In R. L. Schiefelbusch and L. L. Lloyd (Eds.), *Language Perspectives: Acquisition, Retardation, and Intervention*. Baltimore: University Park Press, 1974.

Morehead, D. M., and Morehead, A. E. (Eds.), *Normal and Deficient Child Language*. Baltimore: University Park Press, 1976.

Morris, C. *Signs, Language, and Behavior*. Englewood Cliffs, N. J.: Prentice-Hall, 1946.

Muma, J. R. *Language Handbook: Concepts, Assessment, Intervention*. Englewood Cliffs, N.J.: Prentice-Hall, 1978.

Ol'eron, P. *Language and Mental Development*. Hillsdale, N.J.: Erlbaum, 1977.

Osgood, C. "A Behavioristic Analysis of Perception and Language as Cognitive Phenomena." In J. Bruner, and others (Eds.), *Contemporary Approaches to Cognition*. Cambridge, Mass.: Harvard University Press, 1957.

Osofsky, J. D. *Handbook of Infant Development*. New York: Wiley, 1979.

Piaget, J. *The Language and Thought of the Child*. New York: Harcourt, 1926.

Premack, D., "A Functional Analysis of Language." *Journal of Experimental Analysis Behavior*, 1970, *14*, 107–125.

Ramey, C. T., and Mills, P. J. "Mother-Infant Interaction Patterns as a Function of Rearing Conditions." Paper presented at the Society for Research in Child Development, Denver, Colorado, April, 1975.

Ramey, C. T., Sparling, J. J., and Wasik, B. H. "Creating Social Environments to Facilitate Language Development." In R. L. Schiefelbusch and D. D. Bricker (Eds.), *Early Language Intervention.* Baltimore: University Park Press, forthcoming.

Rees, N. S. "Pragmatics of Language: Application to Normal and Disordered Language Development." In R. L. Schiefelbusch (Ed.), *Bases of Language Intervention.* Baltimore: University Park Press, 1978.

Rogers-Warren, A., and Warren, S. *Ecological Perspectives in Behavior Analysis.* Baltimore: University Park Press, 1978.

Ruder, K. F. "Planning and Programming for Language Intervention." In R. L. Schiefelbusch (Ed.), *Bases of Language Intervention.* Baltimore: University Park Press, 1978.

Ruder, K. F., and Smith, M. D. "Issues in Language Training." In R. L. Schiefelbusch and L. L. Lloyd (Eds.), *Language Perspectives: Acquisition, Retardation, and Intervention.* Baltimore: University Park Press, 1974.

Rumbaugh, D. M. (Ed.). *Language Learning by a Chimpanzee.* New York: Academic Press, 1977.

Schaeffer, B. "Spontaneous Language Through Signed Speech." In R. L. Schiefelbusch (Ed.), *Nonspeech Language and Communication.* Baltimore: University Park Press, 1979.

Schiefelbusch, R. L. (Ed.). *Bases of Language Intervention.* Baltimore: University Park Press, 1978a.

Schiefelbusch, R. L. *Language Intervention Strategies.* Baltimore: University Park Press, 1978b.

Schiefelbusch, R. L., and Hollis, J. H. "A General System for Nonspeech Language." In R. L. Schiefelbusch (Ed.), *Nonspeech Language and Communication.* Baltimore: University Park Press, 1979.

Schiefelbusch, R. L., and Lloyd, L. L. (Eds.), *Language Perspectives: Acquisition, Retardation, and Intervention.* Baltimore: University Park Press, 1974.

Schumaker, J. B., and Sherman, J. A. "Training Generative Verb Usage by Imitation and Reinforcement Procedure." *Journal of Applied Behavior Analysis,* 1970, *3,* 273–287.

Schumaker, J. B., and Sherman, J. A. "Parent as Intervention Agent." In R. L. Schiefelbusch (Ed.), *Language Intervention Strategies.* Baltimore: University Park Press, 1978.

Shane, H. C., "Approaches to Assessing the Communication of Nonoral Persons." In R. L. Schiefelbusch (Ed.), *Nonspeech Language and Communication.* Baltimore: University Park Press, 1979.

Sievers, D. J., and Essa, S. H. "Language Development in Institutionalized Children." *American Journal of Mental Deficiency,* 1961, *66,* 413–420.

Skinner, B. F. *Verbal Behavior.* New York: Appleton-Century-Crofts, 1957.

Spradlin, J. E. "Language and Communication of Mental Defectives." In N. Ellis (Ed.), *Handbook of Mental Deficiency.* New York: McGraw-Hill, 1963a.

Spradlin, J. E. "Assessment of Speech and Language of Mentally Retarded Children: The Parsons Language Sample." In R. L. Schiefelbusch (Ed.), *Language Studies of Mentally Retarded Children. Journal of Speech and Hearing Disorders, Monograph Suppl. No. 10,* 1963b, pp. 8–31.

Spreen, O. "Language Functions in Mental Retardation, A Review II. Language in Higher Level Performance." *American Journal of Mental Deficiency,* 1965, *70,* 351–362.

Staats, A. W. "Behaviorism and Cognitive Theory in the Study of Language: A Neopsycholinguistic Theory." In R. L. Schiefelbusch and L. L. Lloyd (Eds.), *Language Perspectives: Acquisition, Retardation, and Intervention,* Baltimore: University Park Press, 1974.

Stevenson, J. *Basic Behavioral Development.* Unpublished manuscript, 1962.

Sugarman-Bell, S. "Some Organizational Aspects of Pre-Verbal Communication." In I. Markova (Ed.), *The Social Context of Language.* New York: Wiley, 1978.

Thoman, E. B. "Infant Development Within the Mother-Infant Relationship." In E. Quilligan and N. Kretchmer (Eds.), *Perinatal Medicine.* New York: Wiley, 1978.

Tjossem, T. D. *Intervention Strategies for High Risk Infants and Young Children.* Baltimore: University Park Press, 1976.

Trehub, S. E., Bull, D., and Schneider, B. A. "Infant Speech and Nonspeech Perception: A Review and Evaluation." In R. L. Schiefelbusch and D. D. Bricker (Eds.), *Early Language Intervention.* Baltimore: University Park Press, forthcoming.

Waryas, C. L., and Stremel-Campbell, K. "Grammatical Training for the Language-Delayed Child: A New Perspective." In R. L. Schiefelbusch (Ed.), *Language Intervention Strategies.* Baltimore: University Park Press, 1978.

Wollman, D. H. "A Presymbolic Training Program." In R. L. Schiefelbusch (Ed.), *Nonspeech Language and Communication.* Baltimore: University Park Press, 1979.

Wulz, S. V., and Hollis, J. H. "Application of Manual Signing to the Development of Reading Skills." In R. L. Schiefelbusch and J. H. Hollis (Eds.), *Language Intervention from Ape to Child.* Baltimore: University Park Press, 1979.

Richard L. Schiefelbusch is university professor, director of the Bureau of Child Research, University of Kansas.

*The emphasis of this chapter is on the need to re-orient language
training towards an ecologically sound system focusing on
the inclusion of family members as teachers and the use of
everyday activities for encouraging functional communication.*

An Ecological Approach
to Language Intervention

Gerald Mahoney
Emy Lu Weller

In almost every aspect of human functioning ranging from politics to business
and from philosophy to education, there have been attempts to redefine what
we are doing and the goals that we hope to achieve in terms of our social and
physical environment. The field of language intervention has not been
immune from ecological considerations. For example, a major recurring problem related to language intervention efforts has been the failure of children to
incorporate language responses learned in intervention settings to their spontaneous communication. It has been argued that this problem may be related
to the fact that language intervention procedures and the theories upon which
they are based have been conceptualized and developed with little regard for
the ecological processes involved in the normal development of language
(Mahoney, 1975; Mahoney and Seeley, 1976).

While few dispute the value of understanding the ecology of language
development and the usefulness of incorporating these considerations into
language intervention programs, few language programs have been developed
that totally represent this approach. This situation reflects partly the limited
knowledge that we currently have regarding the ecology of language acquisition as well as a reluctance to abandon language intervention approaches of

known value in favor of language intervention approaches of unknown value. However, until intervention procedures based upon an ecological model are developed and demonstrated to be effective, ecological considerations are little more than rhetoric, and as such, the potential of these considerations will fail to have any significant impact on language training procedures. With the strong conviction that ecological considerations are crucial for effective language intervention, we attempt in this chapter to define an ecological approach to language intervention, and to develop specific implications of this approach for language intervention.

Definition of an Ecological Approach

The ecological approach may be defined as a series of principles and procedures which are designed primarily for maximizing the social communication efficiency of language-delayed children. Intervention procedures are, therefore, neither designed to develop language as a behavior which has inherent value out of social context, nor as a symbolic tool for increased cognitive functioning. Rather, language is developed primarily as a means for effective communication, and language training procedures are evaluated according to the degree to which they promote communication effectiveness.

We have derived four basic principles from the theoretical and research literature regarding the relationship between language and communication which we will use as the bases for the major considerations regarding ecological language training procedures. These principles represent a wide range of research findings and theoretical perspectives which can be interpreted as supporting the position that social communication is central to the development of language. The first principle is that language intervention procedures should closely simulate the naturally occurring processes of language acquisition. This principle is based upon several assumptions. The first is that the ability to acquire language has evolved through the process of natural selection which appears to be an efficient means for learning language (De Laguna, 1927). While it is possible that more efficient methods for acquiring language may be developed artificially, it is nevertheless important to capitalize on the wisdom of naturally occurring processes. Second, it is assumed that the process of language acquisition is a multifaceted phenomenon which can be conceptualized broadly in terms of its content, context, and the social processes which occur during its acquisition. Each of these dimensions follow general rule-governed developmental sequences. Third, the simulation of naturally occurring language development processes requires that language curricula and teaching methods parallel and magnify language learning processes as they have been observed in nature. The failure of language-delayed children to acquire language under natural language learning conditions does not undermine their value as valid guidelines for intervention procedures.

The second principle is that language is a sophisticated means of communication which has evolved from lower forms of communication. This conceptualization of language is consistent with the speech acts model of language (Searle, 1969) which stresses the function of language (how language is used) rather than its structure (the organization of language) as the central dimension. Language is conceived in terms of the message which the speaker intends to communicate and the interpretation of that message by the listener. Language generally begins with the ability of children to convey and receive messages nonverbally. As children develop language the structural complexity of messages expands although the precise meaning of messages may continue to be related to nonverbal communication cues and to the context of the communication cues and to the context of the communication exchange. According to this ecological principle, language training procedures are initiated with primitive forms of nonverbal communication and are always conducted within the context of communication exchanges.

The third principle is that natural language models, particularly parents, participate actively in their children's language acquisition. Maternal involvement begins with establishment of nonverbal and primitive conversational patterns with children. This includes early mother-child play routines which parallel the structure of language, and gaze behavior or other mother-child directional cues which help them focus on common referents. Maternal language has several qualities which may facilitate children's language development. These include accentuated intonation patterns, simplified syntactic structures, frequent repetitions, restricted vocabulary, and reference only to objects and events within children's perceptual field. The involvement of parents in language development is, therefore, more comprehensive than some behavioral theories of language acquisition suggest. While parents occasionally reinforce appropriate language responses and frequently model language behavior, they also serve to establish early communication patterns with their children and gradually expand these patterns into more effective means of communication. Because of the unique communication opportunities between parents and their children, parents should be principal resources for implementing language training procedures.

The fourth principle is that the acquisition of language requires the active participation of children. It begins in the preverbal stage with an infant's selective attention to language stimuli and continues throughout the entire period of language development. Children's language learning activities include: initiating social communication; formulating hypotheses regarding the nature and structure of language; practicing of intonation patterns, vocabulary, and linguistic structure spontaneously; imitating selective aspects of language addressed to them; determining the relationship between the utterances and intentions of speakers; and asking questions about language. Since children's active language participation is an integral aspect of language acquisition, intervention should be designed to elicit and increase children's use of these language learning activities.

Implications for Language Intervention

The implications of the four ecological principles for language intervention may be described in terms of the context for language training, the content of the material used during intervention, and the implementation of language training procedures. In the following section each of these key areas will be described as extensions of the four ecological principles.

Context

There are several options for selecting the location for conducting language intervention. For example, language training may occur in a language therapist's office, in a classroom, in a child's home, or in a combination of these places. The location of a language training program profoundly influences the nature of the communication situation in which children develop language. The context influences factors such as who does the language training, who is present during language training, the form and content of the messages communicated, the objects used, and the time of training. For example, if language training occurs in the office of the language therapist, the therapist usually becomes the principle language trainer; only the therapist and child are present during language training; the messages communicated are unidimensional with the child primarily responding to the intentions of the therapist; the topic of the language lesson is often centered on objects and pictures that are unfamiliar or uninteresting to the child; and language training is conducted for fixed periods of time, one or two days a week. If, on the other hand, language training occurs in the classroom, the teacher may be the principal language trainer; several other children may be present during language training; the topic of the language lesson is designated by specific language curriculum or by predetermined behavioral objectives; language training is often constrained and artificial with the teacher attempting to elicit and reinforce specific language responses which are centered on objects provided in a language kit; and language training is provided daily for a fixed period of time during the designated language period. The six factors—where language training occurs, who does the language training, the people present during language training, the form and content of the messages, the objects used, and the time of language training—are all part of the context for language intervention. According to the ecological approach the acquisition of language optimally occurs within the context of familiar social exchanges in which both children and their language models participate actively. For very young children this context is the home; for preschool and school-aged children it is the home and school, with the home playing a less important role over time; while for older language delayed persons, it is the vocational setting and place of residence.

In home settings mothers may assume the role of primary language trainers, although over time, fathers and siblings become increasingly influential language models. The topics of most communicative exchanges revolve around the familiar activities, routines, objects, and environmental cues of the home. Both children and their language models take turns initiating and responding to communicative intentions, to comment on events, to signal, for activities to occur, to protest actions, to ask for information, to request objects, or to request actions from others. The form of these communicative exchanges varies with the changing intentions of children and their language models. Similarly, the objects on which communication centers are a function of the activity in which the children and their language models engage. These periodic social exchanges throughout the day provide optimal contexts for language training to occur.

Invaluable opportunities for communicative exchanges between children and their mothers occur frequently in typical home settings. Children and mothers actively interact during familiar feeding, toileting, dressing, and play routines. Children become familiar with the objects and environmental cues that accompany these routines. For example, they begin to understand that when they hear the phrase, "Time to eat!" within the context of Mom cooking in the kitchen, Dad setting the table, Sister pointing to a familiar high chair as she holds up a bib, and Brother arriving home from baseball practice — that dinner is forthcoming. The redundancy of cues in the environment is particularly useful in helping children determine the meaning of language.

As children become familiar with their relationships with people, objects, routines, activities, and other daily environmental cues, they gain more opportunities for social communication. They may begin to communicate their anticipation of certain events which are indicated by multiple environmental cues. For example, children may walk to the door and say "bye-bye" when they see their mother get her coat, keys, and purse. They may begin to signal to cause events to occur. Children may learn that if they knock on the refrigerator door their father will give them a drink. They may learn that if they start clapping their hands their sister will join them in pat-a-cake. Children's first experiences with using language for communication purposes are also intimately tied to their active interaction with their environment. Through their experiences with the familiar objects and events in their daily environment, children gain an experiental base from which they can begin to communicate their intentions, thoughts, and needs and from which they can learn to respond to the intentions, thoughts, and needs of others.

The daily environment also provides children with many opportunities to use what is learned in one situation in different contexts. Such opportunities occur when the inherent structure of daily routines is altered because of situational variations. For example, there may be a definite post-dinner routine established in the home in which everyone helps clean up the dinner dishes and then watches television. This basic routine may vary when guests come to dinner, changes occur in household repsonsibilities, or television viewing is substituted with another activity such as going to a movie. The context of these changes provides children the opportunity to say words learned in familiar situations in new settings with different people. For example, children who are learning to say "up" to be lifted into their mother's lap may learn to use the same term to request to be lifted into their father's lap, onto a car seat, or into a high chair. Likewise, children who hear a sharp "No!" from their mothers when they are about to throw a cup on the floor, or from their brother when they attempt to turn off the television, gradually learn to stop their activity when given that verbal command.

The commitment to conducting language intervention in contexts which are familiar to children requires more than adapting procedures devised in therapists' offices. It requires consideration of the complexity of children's familiar environments and a careful identification of the routines and activities that could lead to optimal episodes of language instruction. These considerations entail an understanding of the given context from the children's perspective, including information regarding the objects or events which are most interesting to them, when and where they are most likely to initiate communication, and the people with whom they communicate most frequently.

Content

The content selected for an ecological language curriculum does not depart radically from the content of many contemporary language intervention programs. The major difference is in the emphasis on establishing language as a communicative behavior. While in most language programs, the various language components such as semantics, syntax, and phonology are viewed as a means for establishing communication, in the ecological approach, communication is viewed as the source for the development of these language components. Communication is, therefore, considered the core content area of language intervention from which other components of language must evolve.

Although the content for the curriculum is derived from theory and research regarding language development, the developmental literature is not viewed as a prescription for absolute sequences of behavior. Rather the literature is assumed to specify the relative probability that certain aspects of language may be learned while children function at given levels of language development. Consequently, those behaviors reported to occur at certain levels of language development are viewed as highly probable language intervention targets for children who function at that level of language development. Behaviors which are not typically learned by children at certain levels of language development may also be intervention targets although the probability of success is considerably lower for these behaviors.

Each of the content areas for language training will be described below in the order in which they first appear developmentally. These content areas should continue to be developed as training for subsequent content areas is initiated. Therefore, the initiation of the training of a higher order content area does not mark the termination of training in lower order content areas. Furthermore, the skill or language form which is developed in the higher order content area should not exceed the range of intentions which have been communicated from lower order content areas. This reflects the general language development principle that new language forms are used to express meanings which have been expressed previously in established communication forms.

Nonverbal Communication. The most fundamental content area for language intervention is nonverbal communication. Children must have a basic understanding of the general principles of communication; in other words, that communication is a dyadic process in which intentions may be transmitted or exchanged by the use of signs, symbols, or events, prior to learning formal linguistic behaviors. This requires that children have intentions to communicate, that they recognize that these intentions may be expressed by means of signals, gestures, or symbols, and that they perceive that a message is or is not producing the intended effect on the listener. Similarly, children must also come to understand that when speakers emit given gestures, signals, or symbols, these represent their intentions.

Language learners must also learn the rules of communication discourse. These include, but are not limited to, knowledge that speakers and listeners can take turns in the communicative process (when the speaker stops communicating, the listener can assume the role of the speaker), and knowledge that speakers and listeners may either respond to the content of each other's message or may introduce a new topic into the flow of conversation.

Both specific intentions and general classes of intentions may be communicated nonverbally. Nonverbal signals which refer to particular instances, objects, or events and are the precursors to words and phrases can be classified as specific intentions. Nonverbal signals which express broad communicative functions such as expressions of feelings, commands, requests, and comments can be classified as general intentions. General intentions are the precursors to the pragmatic functions of language which have been identified by Dore (1975) as *primary speech acts*. Most of the pragmatic functions identified in early child language are believed to originate in nonverbal communication. Consequently, curricula for nonverbal communication should include activities which lead children to differentiate receptive and expressive communicative functions in the nonverbal mode.

Generally, the content for nonverbal communication must include activities for teaching the fundamentals of communication, including the use of differentiated signals to communicate specific intentions, the use of signals to communicate general communicative functions, and the rule of communicative discourse. Attempts to teach verbal communication to children should not begin until children demonstrate some competence in each of these nonverbal communication skills. Furthermore, initial verbal communication training should map onto children's existing nonverbal communication system.

Preverbal Communication. A second component of a language intervention curriculum is preverbal communication. Preverbal communication is the systematic use of idiosyncratic vocalizations or intonation patterns to represent specific objects, feelings, or events. In preverbal communication children may use their own vocalizations as if they were words or phrases. While the goal of language intervention is clearly not to sustain or increase the frequency of idiosyncratic speech, the use of this form of communication reflects the development of children's ability to express their intentions, and as such ought to be encouraged or reinforced. Although it is unnecessary to teach idiosyncratic vocalizations, it is important to identify those sounds or intonation patterns which children use spontaneously so that these vocalizations may serve as a basis for training new words. It is important to recognize that even though preverbal vocalizations are inconsistent with adult words, they have communicative value insofar as listeners can easily identify their meanings. From the children's point of view, they may represent sophisticated attempts to communicate.

Initial Utterances and Semantic Relations. Two parameters of language are key considerations in the development of children's initial one word utterances. One is to focus on words that are consistent with the range of children's specific communicative intentions. Children's initial one-word utterances should refer to objects, actions, attributes, or object relationships with which they have demonstrated competence in nonverbal communication. For example, if children play with an object such as a comb appropriately, through symbolic play, combing the hair of a doll, or combing their own hair, or if children use nonverbal communication to request or comment on a comb, then "comb" is an excellent candidate as an initial verbal target. If, on the other hand, children are unfamiliar with various objects, persons, or events or do not attempt to communicate about them nonverbally, then words representing those objects should not be selected as a part of the initial instructional vocabulary.

The second parameter is that children's initial one-word utterances should be taught according to the general communicative functions which they have demonstrated in the nonverbal mode. For some children, labeling ("That is a car.") may not be among the general functions which compose their early repertoire of communicative behavior. Teaching words as a labeling activity to these children should be avoided entirely. However, even those children who do label at an early age also use communication for other general functions such as feelings, requests, or commands. While it is appropriate to teach words as labels to these children, it is also important that emphasis be placed on developing initial one-word utterances within the context of other communicative functions.

In general, the initial words for teaching children should be selected so that they match their nonverbal communication abilities. This requires that word selection be individualized to the children's own abilities or interests but does not require either that word selection be derived from developmental data or that word selection be designed to develop specified functional language behavior.

The initial development of multiple word utterances reflects the extension of children's intentional behavior to comment or reflect on the relationships between objects and events in their environment. This development not only reflects children's increasing sensitivity and awareness of their environment, but also reflects their awareness that some of these relationships may be communicated more effectively through word order and other formal semantic devices. The semantic relational rules, such as agent-action, action-object, object-location, and so forth, which account for most children's initial multiple word utterances (Brown, 1973) are consistent with the ecological viewpoint that language evolves from communication, since they are thought to evolve from children's intentional behavior. These rules are important curricular guides for training multiple word utterances because they provide a conceptualization which ties the transition from primitive verbal utterances to formal grammatical utterances with the development of children's intentional behavior. Semantic relational rules, however, may not necessarily specify a language training curriculum which differs radically from curricula generated from formal syntactic descriptions of early two- and three- word utterances. Rather, the primary value of these rules is that they provide a vehicle for deriving formal grammatical structures from children's intentional behavior.

Syntax. While many have felt that the development of syntax should be the primary goal for language intervention, the ecological approach deviates significantly from this emphasis. Syntax is viewed as an important development for increasing the efficiency of language communication but is not considered as a language intervention goal which has value independent of the development of communication. The use of appropriate grammatical structure enables speakers to communicate intentions with greater clarity to others. Communicative intentions are viewed as the core component of language and syntax, and the use of appropriate linguistic structure is a means for increasing the efficiency of communicating these intentions verbally.

Given this perspective on syntax, the teaching of language structure becomes the final, rather than initial, component of language intervention. In addition, syntax is not taught as a behavior which has inherent value but rather only as a behavior which can lead to the production of more efficient communication. Natural developmental sequences are used to identify a syntactic curriculum, but since the teaching of syntax focuses on the relationship between syntax and communication, communicative contexts also influence the selection of the syntactic structures that are taught.

The Process of Language Intervention

The emphasis of the ecological approach is primarily on the process rather than the content for language intervention. How language training procedures are implemented is the most crucial consideration to this approach. In the following section we will describe how the ecological approach might be implemented by focusing on three components of language intervention programs: the goal for language intervention: the roles of language therapists, language models, and children in intervention; and the use of reinforcement in intervention. Careful attention to each of these components is viewed as a prerequisite to the implementation of this approach.

The Goal of Language Intervention. The basic goal of language intervention is to increase children's communication efficiency within the context of social interactions. Communication efficiency refers to the ability to relay and receive messages appropriately and efficiently in interpersonal situations. Appropriate communication occurs when children use language behavior that fits the expectations of those with whom they interact. Children gradually learn that it is not appropriate to have a tantrum in the aisle of a grocery store, to speak loudly in a library, or to tell someone that he is ugly. Effective communication occurs when children are able to understand and use more complex words and sentence structure, they become better able to express their feelings, control the behavior of others, inform others of experiences, participate in ritualized or formal social situations, and participate in imaginative play — functions felt to characterize the dominant uses of communication in contemporary life.

The goal of communication efficiency can be attained only within the context of social interaction and is much more comprehensive than the isolated goals of increased vocabulary, use of specific sentence structure, and precise articulation in a speech therapy room. Language intervention must, therefore, be reconceptualized away from a previous emphasis on what children express regardless of the communicative situation to an emphasis on how children express their intentions within the contexts of specific social situations.

The Roles of Individuals Involved in Language Training. In traditional language intervention programs, language therapists have been the principal agents for conducting language intervention. They have typically worked with children in one-to-one situations using techniques of imitation, shaping, modeling, and positive reinforcement. This role has emerged because language development has been viewed as evolving from within the child and because language training is thought to require the specialized skills of a speech therapist. However, if language is thought of primarily as a social interactive behavior which evolves from the context of children interacting with parents and other primary caregivers, and if the goal of language training is to increase the communicative efficiency of children, it becomes apparent that persons who have close social relationships to children must assume a greater role in language training and that the role of language therapists must be redefined.

Language therapists must assume a role of mediating the communicative interaction between children and their language models. This role includes the dual functions of teacher and program monitor. As teachers, therapists must provide parents and other language models developmental information regarding the content and sequence of the communication and language behaviors acquired by children. They need to specify the patterns of interaction which facilitate the acquisition of these behaviors. Therapists must sensitize parents to reflect on what they understand about their children's communication and to be aware of new developments in their children's nonverbal, pragmatic, semantic, and syntactic behavior.

In addition to teaching basic information, language therapists should periodically monitor the communicative interaction between children and their language models in two ways. First, language therapists can demonstrate proper patterns of communicative interaction by interacting with the children themselves. Second, language therapists can provide corrective feedback to language models either while the language model and child are interacting, or by critiquing a video recording of their interaction. This monitoring of language interaction can include two methods of feedback to language models. The first is to review and explore with language models the range and quality of their children's communication repertoire and to examine the nature of the language models' response to this communication system. The second is to assist language models in adapting their communication and language to the communicative competence of their children.

Language therapists serve as consultants rather than as primary language models. They provide both emotional and instructional support to parents and others who serve as primary language models. This support includes developing an awareness in language models of the parents' critical role in language intervention, encouraging them to sustain this role when they lose confidence or motivation, providing them with information and suggestions when they encounter communication problems with their child, and periodically evaluating the progress of the children.

With language therapists assuming the role of a consultant, parents, primary caregivers, siblings, teachers, and others who have frequent social contact with the children must assume the role of primary language teacher. As primary language teachers they are reponsible for implementing language instruction as social interactions with children occur. They should be sensitive to their children's level of communicative functioning, and they should have realistic expectations of the range of communication behaviors that their children are most likely to develop.

Language models serve a variety of critical functions. They are communication models. As children progress through the various stages of communication competence, language models must learn to use past accumulated information about their children to attempt to determine the children's intentions, and they must become aware of how their own communication affects children. Sensitivity to children's communication requires careful attention to the nature of emitted signals, as well as efforts to encourage children to increase their level of communication activity. Awareness of the effects of their own communication on children requires language models to modify their communication to a level which is commensurate with children's communicative competence so that maximum responsiveness from children is elicited.

Language models must also function as communication catalysts. That is, they must devise environmental events and familiar or novel social interactions which elicit spontaneous communication from children. They are responsible for providing positive emotional and motivational support which stimulates children to actively engage in social communication.

Language models will undoubtedly encounter numerous problems in their efforts to facilitate their children's communication development. Since they are not language experts, it is their responsibility to seek out expert information and advice which might help them in their interactions with their children. It is crucial that language models acknowledge the serious nature of their responsibility, and that they respond to this responsibility by aggressively seeking information from various resources available in the community.

Language-delayed children, the most important members of the intervention team, are viewed primarily as active communicators. At every level of intellectual functioning, children are assumed to have fundamental needs to communicate their intentions to others. The task of language intervention is to help them discover and develop more efficient communication skills. They are expected to increase their rate of communicative development, however, primarily because of their own active processing of information rather than because of the direct influence of the language environment on them.

Because of this active role which children must assume in developing language, the ecological approach places little emphasis on requiring children to respond repeatedly to highly structured language learning tasks such as sustained sequences of elicited imitation or sustained responding to demands and questions. While verbal imitation and verbal responses are occasionally used as language teaching strategies, overuse of these strategies could result in the failure to elicit children's intentional behavior and could make children passive language learners.

In lieu of these strategies, ecological language training episodes could occur during those daily social situations in which children communicate spontaneously or during contrived communication episodes where the communication context has been structured by the language model in a way that either creates a need for children to communicate or sustains prolonged episodes of communication. Contrived communication episodes could include activities such as cooperative play in which children have an active role in sustaining the play episodes, communication games in which the children must direct the behavior of the other to complete the task, or structured daily routines such as bathing, eating, or dressing in which children are required to initiate communication as a prerequisite to fulfilling their needs.

Since intervention is based on two-way communication between children and their language model, the quality of children's responses to communication episodes should partly determine the content for language instruction. Consequently, if language models introduce a communication episode in which children show no interest, the topic of the episode is inappropriate for the children at that time and other episodes of apparent interest to the children should be substituted.

The topics for communication episodes could be selected by either responding to topics which children have spontaneously communicated, by increasing the communication demands of communicative contexts in which children have previously participated, or by creating new episodes based on topics in which the children show interest. In all cases the communication episode must elicit and sustain the role of children as active communicators.

The Use of Reinforcement. For children to increase their communication efficiency, they must not only learn specific nonverbal behaviors; they must also learn the relationship between those behaviors and the message which they intend to communicate. For example, to use the word "car" as an effective communication signal, children must understand the relationship between that word and their own intention to communicate about an automobile. Therefore, in language intervention, the goal of reinforcement is to encourage children to express their intentions through words or gestures. This requires that children simultaneously intend to communicate about an object or event and emit language behavior which signifies that object or event in order to receive positive reinforcement. Several types of consequent events, such as social praise or various tangible reinforcers, may increase the frequency of specific language behaviors. Many of these reinforcers, however, may actually distract children from understanding the communicative significance of their language. For example, if children receive tangible reinforcers such as candy for correctly saying "kitty" when a picture of a kitten is presented, rather than learning that the word "kitty" is an effective linguistic device for communicating "I want the kitty," the children may actually be learning that one way of getting candy is to say "kitty" whenever they see a representation of a kitten. If this is the actual substance of what children learn, it is unlikely that they will say "kitty" in contexts where candy reinforcement is unavailable, since from their perspective in such contexts, correctly labeling a picture of a kitten has no functional consequences. Consequently, although the use of tangible reinforcers and social praise is effective at increasing the frequency of subsequent language behavior, with the exception of situations where children request candy or affection, such reinforcers signify no apparent relationship between the language behavior and intentions of the children.

Careful attention to the nature of the consequences used in language training can facilitate the process of establishing the relationship between the language behavior and intentions of children. If language is viewed fundamentally as a means for social communication, two criteria must be used for selecting reinforcers. The first is that the reinforcer increase the frequency with which children emit language behavior in subsequent appropriate situations. The second is that the reinforcer link the children's language behavior to their intentions. If children attempt to produce language primarily as means for communicating their intention, then any indication from the listener that their intention has been understood is likely to be perceived by the children as a rewarding subsequent event and should, therefore, increase the frequency of that behavior. Similarly, the failure of the listener to respond to children's language behavior according to their intention may be viewed by the children as a negative consequence and, subsequently, should lead to a decrease in the occurrence of that behavior as a communicative response.

According to the ecological approach, reinforcement remains an important component of language intervention. The behavior which is reinforced, however, is the appropriate relationship between the language behavior and intention of the child, and the reinforcer is any subsequent event which indicates to the child that he has effectively communicated what he intended. The criteria that reinforced behavior include the intention as well as the language behavior of children again underscores the necessity of conducting language intervention in contexts where children are more likely to communicate spontaneously. It also requires that language models are sensitive and responsive to the communication signals of children. To force children to emit language responses in structured settings without regard to the intention of the children would, according to this perspective, fail to establish functional communication behavior. Reinforcers which link the language behavior to children's intentions may include ecologically valid responses such as responding appropriately to children's requests, sustaining topics of conversation which children initiate, or by otherwise communicating to children either verbally or nonverbally that their message was received.

Summary

In this chapter we have presented a brief perspective on an ecological approach to language intervention. We have defined the ecological approach as one in which social communication is the core component of language intervention. Four basic principles for language intervention were derived from language development theory and research, each of which supports the central role of communication in language development. From these principles we generated implications regarding the context of language intervention, the content for language intervention, and the actual implementation of ecological language intervention strategies.

We have argued that the context in which language intervention occurs profoundly influences factors such as who is the principal language teacher, how many people are present during language training, the form and content of messages used for intervention, and the time during which language training occurs. If language intervention is conducted in children's familiar social environment, then parents and others who share close social relationships with children may become primary language trainers. Language training will focus on objects, routines, and people who are familar to the children, and language intervention is likely to occur throughout the day as children engage in spontaneous social communication.

Since the ecological approach is based on the assumption that language evolves from lower forms of communication, then communication becomes the primary content area for language training. Language intervention, therefore, begins with nonverbal forms of communication and gradually introduces linguistic responses into children's communication repertoire. Each linguistic behavior is taught primarily as a tool for increasing children's social communication efficiency.

The implementation of the ecological approach requires a primary emphasis on the goal of increasing children's communication efficiency. It also requires that the roles of people involved in intervention be defined carefully. Language therapists or speech pathologists become consultants to others who serve as primary language models. They mediate the relationship between language models and children by providing them both emotional and instructional support. Primary language models are parents, relatives, teachers, and others who have close social contact with the children. They assume primary responsibility for implementing children's intervention programs. They conceptualize language-delayed children primarily as active communicators, and intervention efforts are geared toward capitalizing on episodes of spontaneous communication. Reinforcement is a major component of language intervention, but the behavior which is reinforced is the relationship between children's language and their intention to communicate, while reinforcers include any subsequent event which provides children feedback linking their language behavior to their intention.

References

Brown, R. *A First Language: The Early Stages.* Cambridge, Mass.: Harvard University Press, 1973.

De Laguna, G. *Speech: Its Function and Development.* New Haven, Conn.: Yale University Press, 1927.

Dore, J. "Holophrases, Speech Acts, and Language Universals." *Journal of Child Language,* 1975, *2,* 21–40.

Mahoney, G. "An Ethological Approach to Delayed Language Acquisition." *American Journal of Mental Deficiency,* 1975, *80,* 139–148.

Mahoney, G., and Seeley, P. "The Role of the Social Agent in Language Acquisition: Implications for Language Intervention." In N. R. Ellis (Ed.), *International Review of Research in Mental Retardation.* Vol. 8. New York: Academic Press, 1976.

Searle, J. *Speech Acts: An Essay in the Philosophy of Language.* Cambridge, Mass.: Cambridge University Press, 1969.

Gerald Mahoney is an assistant professor of Special Education at the University of California, Los Angeles.

Emy Lu Weller is the director of the Learning Assistance Center, Pasadena City College.

In developing effective language training models for young handicapped children, language interventionists must consider the perspective that the origins of language may lie in early sensorimotor and social-communicative activities.

An Intervention Approach for Communicatively Handicapped Infants and Young Children

Diane D. Bricker
Laurel Carlson

The dramatic rise in the development of early intervention programs for young handicapped children has resulted in increased demands for effective intervention models, training strategies, and educational materials. Training materials to meet the needs of this increasingly younger population have been particularly scarce in the area of preverbal communication and early language skills. Many language training programs begin with the assumption that the child already has, at least, a minimal comprehension and production repertoire, with the primary objectives being the expansion and refinement of those skills. Such programs are often inappropriate for both the very young or severely impaired child. In response to this deficit the present chapter has two purposes. First, to suggest a number of principles that should be applied when undertaking communicative interaction with young handicapped children. These principles have been synthesized from the available literature as well as our own work. Second, to suggest the necessary content of early preverbal communication and early language intervention and the sequence in which that content might most successfully be taught.

Philosophy of Intervention

As Bruner (1975, p. 276) suggests, "The purpose of language is communication," a perspective often overlooked among the flurry of models, structures and analyses detailing the intricacies of child language. Yet for all this esoteric activity, the goal for the interventionist must remain assisting handicapped children in acquiring the most adaptable, generalizable and acceptable communication skills possible. To reach this goal, we believe that intervention programs need direction and regulation by some broad underlying theoretical framework or orientation. We have suggested elsewhere that:

> An underlying theoretical framework should provide cohesiveness and consistency to the program by directing the decision-making process at a number of levels which include (1) the determination of short-term and long-term objectives and priority areas for the child's educational program, (2) the selection of strategies for facilitating acquisition of the established objectives, (3) the selection of appropriate evaluation instruments to assess initial levels of development and monitor change, and (4) the construction, adaptation, or modification of training materials and curricula (Bricker, Seibert, and Casuso, 1980, p. 11).

The framework which we have found most useful is based largely on a developmental approach with some idiosyncratic variations which we have tagged as a developmental-interactive approach. The relevance of this approach to intervention is based on the following assumptions:

- Early developmental processes are so intimately related as to render them often inseparable for educational or training puposes.
- The child and his environment engage in ongoing reciprocal activities which continually influence intervention efforts.
- Behavior changes from simple to complex forms following general but consistent guidelines which provide a set of behavioral targets for intervention.
- Disequilibrium produced by changing environmental demands is necessary for building new adaptive responses.

We believe that sensorimotor, affective and early language behavior are closely related and often inseparable. This premise has implications for intervention programs. It suggests that an intervention approach with young children might be most logically and effectively formulated by coordinating training targets across related domains of behavior, rather than by developing isolated training strands which focus on single behavioral domains. Intervention programs should be designed to affect language, sensorimotor, and affective domains of behavior. For example, teaching a toddler to shake her head affirmatively (1) increases her communicative repertoire, (2) enables her to express her emotional state with more sophistication, and (3) equips her with a convenient response mode for learning conceptual material presented by her teacher. It is our impression that many interventionists proceed in this fashion implicitly. However, we have still observed teachers who compartmentalize their training to the point that it never occurs to them to encourage and reinforce language production apart from the period during the day in which language is taught. It may be that at times the teacher should focus on the development of some specific response, but it seems that organizing and coordinating interventions across related domains makes logical if not empirical sense.

A second theoretical premise for educational intervention is the assertion that development is the result of a complex interactional process between the child and environmental imput (Piaget, 1970). Neither maturational nor environmental variables alone can account for development; rather, one must look to the interaction between the child and his environment. The healthy infant comes equipped with organized reflexes such as sucking, grasping, vocalizing and looking. By interacting with a demanding environment, the infant modifies these basic reflexive responses. Gradually shifting from involuntary to voluntary activation, he becomes capable of active exploration of the physical parameters of his world. Such modifications result in more complex behavior. Environmental interactions allow the infant to gradually build a more sophisticated knowledge of the world by selecting information and fitting it to his current structured organization or understanding. A similar interactive system exists between the child and his social environment — primarily provided by the caregiver during the earliest stages of development. The interactional process between the child and his caregivers accounts for the shaping of socially acceptable affective response forms into the child's repertoire. Without appropriate feedback, the child may not develop socially appropriate smiling, eye contact, and gazing; or establish joint reference and joint actions which appear to provide the basis for more advanced communication exchanges. The importance of interactional or transactional processes to intervention must be underscored.

The general description of normal development during infancy addresses the third premise of our theoretical framework. We believe that developmental hierarchies, composed of a series of sequentially acquired behaviors (for example, from head to trunk to limb control) currently provide the best criteria for establishing objectives for child programming. Such information provides general maps of emerging behavior during the first years of life which in turn specify a framework for not only determining appropriate long-term objectives, but also in determining the most desirable sequence along which the program should proceed. The preverbal communication and early language training content developed using this approach will be presented later in this chapter.

The developmental-interactive framework with its attention to developmental antecedents can also suggest appropriate immediate intervention priorities. As discussed above, sensitivity to relationships among domains of behavior can help the interventionist select targets that are both appropriate within and across domains. For example, many early social and self-help skills require a level of understanding of objects in terms of their social functions (a spoon is for eating, shoes are to wear). To understand these functions, the child must have passed the stage where objects are only sucked, banged or dropped. He must have begun to attend to and discriminate between the unique physical properties of objects before he can begin to perceive their social significance.

Although subject to criticism (Guess, Sailor, and Baer, 1977), the use of logical sequences of development to select patterns of intervention targets for young handicapped children seems justified until more functionally effective strategies emerge. This point has been argued in detail elsewhere (Brinker and Bricker, 1980).

The fourth premise of the developmental-interactive framework emphasizes the use of strategies which provide experiences that conflict with the child's current level of understanding. An important Piagetian principle, "moderate novelty," or just tolerable disequilibrium is critical in the process of development of adaptation. Adaptation occurs when the child is exposed to new environmental inputs which require a change in the existing response repertoire. The facility with which a child learns to adapt existing responses to accommodate new information appears to be influenced by the amount of discrepancy between the novel or more difficult environmental information to be acquired and the current schemes available to the child. If the degree of discrepancy is too great, adaptation does not occur. Similarly, if the degree of discrepancy is too small, the child's interest is not maintained and the process of adapting to this environmental situation stops. The interventionist's tasks are to create a balance between asking too much or asking too little from the child. A young child in the process of acquiring his first words should be asked to request a drink by using a single word ("juice," "drink," "water') rather than accepting only a pointing gesture or demanding the child produce a multiword utterance. Arranging the environment to create a just manageable discrepancy between the child's current skill level and the next level of acquisition is a hallmark of effective intervention.

We believe the framework described above provides both orientation and direction for programs of early language intervention and is necessary to highlight more specific principles of intervention. These principles are described below.

Content of Intervention

It should be apparent that we advocate a broad-based approach to preverbal communication and early language intervention with young handicapped children. Such an approach includes attending to the development of social, affective and sensorimotor behavior when developing a program for young language-delayed children. To organize information from these domains of behavior into a cohesive, useful intervention package is an ambitious undertaking and one that is far from completed (Prutting, 1979). Nonetheless, some tentative formulations have been initiated and are offered below.

In developing the content for intervention we have not deviated from relying on normal acquisition patterns except to become more eclectic in our approach. We are convinced that the development of social/affective forms of behavior deserve our explicit attention. The guidance offered by normal developmental patterns in the formulation of intervention programs is, we believe, useful; although we share the reservations of Guess, Sailor, and Baer (1977) about the applicability of the normal model of development when dealing with more severely handicapped or older handicapped individuals.

There are at least two important issues concerning the use of normal developmental data to provide the content of intervention: deviations in the developmental hierarchy or sequences, and the level of specificity of the hierarchies. If one uses developmental data to attempt to generate a series of training steps that are highly specific, then the applicability and appropriateness across groups of children, particularly handicapped children, is questionable. If, however, one moves to a more general level of analysis, the developmental sequences generated are useful in presenting a series of benchmarks or targets which may be appropriate to include in the repertoires of most young handicapped children. Such developmental sequences or logical sequences, as Baer (1973) describes them, can illuminate training in three ways. First, viewing sequences of relevent domains of behavior (for example, affective, sensorimotor, language) may assist the interventionist in noting points of overlap that may be used to enhance the efficiency of training. Second the progression of responses from simple to more complex, whether linear or branching, should suggest a sequence of training that has a probability of being more effective than armchair selections. Third, the interventionist can gain the perspective of an entire behavioral domain rather than isolated response packages.

Developers of language intervention progams operate from a relatively complete, broad base of understanding about the form and function of language. Unfortunately, many practitioners using these programs lack such breadth and consequently can only view language from the often limited perspective detailed by the program. Providing interventionists with a more global picture of language may help them focus not only on short-term objectives, but perhaps more importantly on the long-term communicative needs of the child. Understanding the communicative functions of language may move teachers and parents toward choosing more functional useful responses. We believe that currently the most appropriate content source for language programs for young handicapped children comes from data on normal acquisition and such information is continuing to grow (deVilliers and deVilliers, 1978;

McLean and Snyder-McLean, 1978). Our strategy, then, is to modify training content to reflect these changes and maintain our reliance on normal developmental processes until objective evidence persuades us otherwise.

When planning the content of a communicative intervention program for the young delayed child, we believe it is useful to recognize the developmental sequence of a set of early social and cognitive (or sensorimotor) factors which appear to serve as prerequisites to, or at the very least correlates of, referential language. Very possibly the wealth of social interactions and sensorimotor experiences in the earliest years of life may prepare a framework from which language is derived. To highlight the significant developmental milestones of these prelanguage capacities, we have found it useful to employ a lattice format. A lattice is analogous to a map in that it provides the directions for moving from place to place (or behavior to behavior). The lattice contained in Figure 1 represents the sequential development of early communicative and correlated sensorimotor behavior. These sequences were generated by examining the recent child language literature along with our own data and experience. Using this information, factors which have been singled out as necessary precursors to early referential language were identified and then aligned as suggested by their occurrence in the nonhandicapped population.

In the sensorimotor domain, the three capacities which correlate consistently with the emergence of language are means-ends, play with objects, and imitation (Bates, 1979). The parallel tracks showing each cognitive factor's sequential development appear on the lower half of the lattice. For example, at three months the infant is capable of approximating sounds made by an adult. Likewise, if a mother imitates a sound her baby is producing, the infant is stimulated to repeat the sound. If the mother continues to imitate her baby, a vocal chain may develop as long as the sounds involved are not changed. At 16 months, however, the infant is capable of producing imitational schemes representing more complex patterns of behavior. At this level of development the child who hears his mother say, "Do you want to go bye-bye?" is capable of reproducing extended portions of the utterance, for example, "Go bye-bye."

For play with objects, there are similar developmental patterns which progress through increasingly complex levels of behavior (Rosenblatt, 1977). At five months the infant touches, waves or bangs objects while at sixteen months he pretends his teddy bear is riding an imaginary horse.

Primitive means-ends may be seen at three months when the infant is surprised by the spectacle he creates for himself as he accidently kicks a motion-activated musical toy placed in his crib. Through a trial and error process which may include arm-flailing and head-turning he discovers the kicking movement necessary to recreate such an interesting result. By the sixteenth month, most babies are actively experimenting with new schemes in an attempt to obtain a desired goal. Placed in a situation where a chair or a box are needed to retrieve an attractive toy from a counter top, the child will

Figure 1. Proposed Sequence of Early Communicative Development

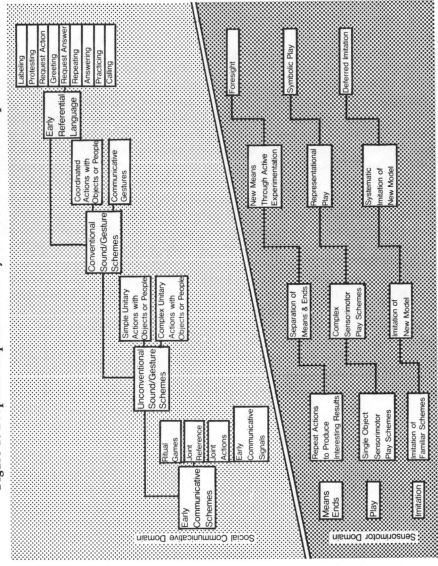

actively seek to obtain the toy by trying out alternative routes to his goal (for example, by first reaching and then moving a chair to climb on). At 24 months the child will be capable of directly obtaining a toy without active experimentation (for example, by moving the chair without first attempting to reach the object).

The sequential development of those behaviors, thought to be more directly related antecedents of referential language, are contained in the upper portion of the lattice in Figure 1.

Early social interactions between the infant and his primary caregivers apparently provide a basis for the development of communication (Bruner, 1975). Through these social exchanges the baby acquires many of the same skills which will be needed when he begins to express his meanings through language. In the first few months of life the young child learns to attend to his mother's speech and in time to wait his turn before responding to her baby talk. By following her gaze the infant is able to discover his mother's focus of attention and mutually establish the same reference point. Likewise, he learns to direct her gaze by fixating his visual focus on objects to which she subsequently attends. Mothers often interpret their infant's interest by assigning meaning to the child's actions and vocal patterns. Attempting to retrieve a dropped teething ring by reaching and vocalizing, an attentive mother will hand the infant the sought-for object. Mothers also make it easier for their infants to interpret signals, both gestural and vocal, by standardizing certain action formats or games (peek-a-boo). Such ritualized activites have a regular structure, giving the baby a chance to anticipate or predict what his mother is going to do next and to align his attention to hers.

Prior to nine months, the baby's vocalizations and primitive gestures appear as unconventionalized schemes; generally their form and purpose (or intent) are not mutually agreed upon by familiar persons (Bates, 1979). During this period, the child's communicative signals often seem oriented more toward direct goal attainment than primary social purposes. When the seven-month-old child plays with objects, his actions tend to be directed solely toward the objects themselves (banging two blocks together and then dropping them into a container) or solely toward a person (vocalizing and reaching toward the adult who then picks him up). Instances in which a person and an object are both involved in a social exchange are rare (Sugarman, 1978). Around nine months, however, significant shifts are seen in the baby's behavior as he starts to coordinate his actions with persons and objects. As his behavior becomes coordinated, the child is essentially demonstrating the capacity for social-tool use employing a person as a means for obtaining an unreachable desired object, and using an object as a means for gaining adult attention. A baby showing coordinated schemes is apt to look and point to a favorite toy beyond his reach, shift his gaze to his mother, vocalize and look back at his goal. If further social bidding is necessary, he might add a tug at her skirt and then mark the toy with a vocal or hand gesture. Coordination is apparent as well in the behavior of a baby who holds a toy horse up to his mother, looks at her, gestures and vocalizes. His mother in turn takes the toy and vocalizes, looking at her child. At the same time that coordination of objects and persons develops, important changes in the baby's communicative signals may be observed. Existing sound/gesture schemes gradually undergo conventionalization. The meaning the baby is trying to convey through his signals is made more explicit and takes a form that is more easily interpretable by others (pointing to desired objects; calling for attention). Thus, by the end of his first year, the infant becomes increasingly capable of integrating his social interactions with object schemes, using conventional gestures, and showing an interest in social interaction for its own sake.

Subsequent to the emergence and elaboration of conventionalized sound/gesture schemes, the child makes the transition to early referential language by using words in a symbolic manner. Conventional communication becomes symbolic when the child realizes that a word (symbol) can be substituted for its referent, and the symbol and its referent are not one and the same. To be considered referential, a word must approximate adult forms phonetically and be used across a variety of contexts ("ca" is used for cars whether referring to Daddy's car or the sound of a car roaring down the street). Once the child has developed referential capacities one word may serve several purposes or uses for the child, including calling, greeting, protesting, labeling or requesting. (Dore, 1975).

Our discussion of the lattice shown in Figure 1 has attempted to highlight the sequential development of some of the social-communicative and sensorimotor behaviors which seem to be significant for the development of early language. It has been suggested that important shifts in sensorimotor and social-interactive capacities have a relationship to the ongoing development of communicative behavior. In terms of intervention, this information should be helpful in pinpointing the language delayed child's communicative stage by orienting the interventionist to the child's level of signal clarity or conventionalization. In addition, we have pointed out those cognitive capacities currently considered most related to language acquisition at the preverbal level. The intactness of these factors should be assessed because of their likely significance for language development.

Context of Intervention

Following completion of his influential project on the classification of exceptional children, Hobbs (1978) concluded that the most effective forms of intervention include all important aspects of the child's ecosystem. If we are to be successful in our training efforts, we must broaden our scope to include all significant elements of the child's life. Earlier we suggested the importance of analyzing language acquisition from an interactive position—that is, a reciprocal feedback system operates between the child and, in particular, his social environment. This position argues for the inclusion of primary care-givers and other family members as necessary participants in the intervention effort with handicapped infants and young children.

Using an ethological model, Mahoney (1975) and Mahoney and Weller (this volume) have suggested that the context of language intervention needs to be broadened to include all aspects of the child's social milieu: "The ethological approach would develop an intervention program based upon the principle that language evolves from the social interaction and nonverbal com-munication system which exist between language-learning children and their primary language models" (Mahoney, 1975, p. 145). The important notion in this position is that language evolves from the early forms of nonverbal com-munication through interaction with the primary caregivers. Development of increasingly more complex language behavior is the result of gradual shifts in the parent's behavior which elicit shifts in the child's behavior. The form and frequency of communicative activity or exchange provided by the primary models is of importance. As a number of investigators have reported, the lan-guage development of children is significantly related to the communicative environment provided by primary caregivers (Nelson, 1973; Tizard, 1974).

The interactive model suggests three practical implications for the con-text of language training. First, family members need to become part of the intervention team. Providing appropriate language models and communica-tive exchanges throughout the handicapped child's day will be dependent upon the skills of the individuals with whom the child has the most contact. The interventionist must be prepared to assist parents in acquiring the necessary skills to become effective change agents with their child. To limit the context of intervention to only professional staff defies logic from two perspectives. First, the primary caregiver, usually the mother, is the one individual with whom the infant spends the most time. If the mother remains ignorant of how to arrange the environment and respond to her child this greatly reduces the number of opportunities that could be used to foster the development of appropriate communicative behavior. Second, through bonding and attach-ment the primary caregiver is usually the infant's most salient social rein-forcer. To ignore this relationship is to ignore a powerful reinforcer for build-ing communicative skills.

The second practical implication for the context of intervention speaks to the issue of training not only across people but across environments. Although training across settings may occur as a natural outgrowth of including the infant's "significant others" in the intervention effort, we will nonetheless emphasize this point separately. By including all settings as potential training environments, one increases the likelihood of expanding the child's language functions and facilitates the generalization of already acquired skills. Expand-ing the training environment to the store, church, or backyard should assist in creating a more adaptable, flexible repertoire for communication between the child and his environment.

The final implication of a practical nature concerns the context of intervention at the task or activity level. It is discouraging to view program after program in which language intervention is conceived and executed as two daily thirty-minute training sessions. The remainder of the day, which could be effectively used to build language skills, is more or less ignored by the interventionist. A more effective format is to superimpose the language instruction over the many training activities and events that occur daily in the child's life. For example, diapering time might be ideal for encouraging vocalizing while child and caregiver are face-to-face. Likewise, feeding activities can be designed to foster the social exchange upon which formal language will later be superimposed.

Structure of Intervention

A growing excitement is evident for early intervention programs. The political pressures (rights of the handicapped, working parents) influencing early intervention are such that the issue seems to be not whether to have these programs but how to structure them to be maximally effective. Intervening early with those children who have significant developmental problems is advisable because initial stages of behavioral development provide the material from which later, more complex levels of behavioral organization evolve. We are convinced that it is efficient and effective to provide a structured intervention program at the point the infant or young child's behavioral repertoire is detected as being consistently delayed or deviant. For many children—particularly those with genetic or organic disabilities— the point of detection may occur during the first year of life (Bricker and Dow, in press). Our first structural principle is to intervene when the problem is detected.

A second structural principle focuses on the breadth of the intervention program. Our view concerning the interrelated nature of early behavior strongly suggests that a program should focus its training efforts across a number of behavioral domains. We have found few handicapped infants with problems that influence only one area of behavior, although this may be a function of the more severely handicapped infants and children with which we work. At the very least, the interventionist needs to be alert to the possibility that a youngster with a language delay may have other behavioral deficiencies that call for remediation as well.

A third structural principle is the need to include the family as a part of the intervention team whenever possible. Most early intervention programs now report the inclusion of parents (Bricker, Seibert, and Scott, in press); however, our concern is oriented toward the nature of that inclusion. Having parents attend meetings, sell cookies to raise money, or talk to civic organizations is admirable but does not constitute the form of involvement we are advocating. We suggest that family members become at least equal partners with the professional staff in the education of their handicapped infant (Turnbull,

1978). For example, with delayed infants, key aspects of the parent-child interaction network could be singled out as a focus for educational programming.

A fourth structural principle in the development of an intervention program is that the form and function of training be child-imposed rather than adult-imposed. Often we have watched a young child vainly attempt to communicate with a teacher who stops the child in order to begin the language training session. Of course, we are not suggesting that teachers be limited only to teaching in unstructured situations, since it is not always possible to rely on the occurrence of natural events to teach specific concepts. Rather, with a little creativity on the part of parents and interventionists, a number of situations arise which can be structured to enhance both the acquisition and generalization of important responses. For example, at snack time the child could be provided with simple choices in which he could communicate the desired food via gesture (pointing), word ("juice"), or gesture/sound sequences (pointing while vocalizing). Natural barriers interferring with progress toward desirable goals may be effectively utilized to build communicative skills. Having the child stop at the doorway before continuing outside could be used to encourage him to vocalize his desire to proceed. After the completion of a meal, leaving the child in his high chair until he produces a gestural or verbal request to "get down" can be an ideal training child-initiated communicative behavior. It must be kept in mind, however, that such a child-focused orientation is clearly less applicable to the severely handicapped who may have an extremely limited response repertoire and who may be almost entirely dependent upon others to arrange the environment and deliver consequences.

We are not advocating a loose, unstructured approach to intervention. Instead, we are recommending a structure and curricular approach that is infinitely modifiable in the hands of a knowledgable interventionist. Rather than developing curricula that provide daily lesson plans, we prefer the strategy of specifying the general content and skills of a domain and the probable sequence in which that content or skill is most readily acquired. We do not dispute the claim that some children will acquire responses in an atypical fashion; nevertheless, we believe that most children follow a relatively predictable route in the acquisition of more and more complex behavior. First knowing the route and then the proper time to modify it with specific children is essential to effective teaching.

Once the content and structure of a program have been chosen, the next question becomes one of implementation. The first step in implementing an instructional program is to determine the level to begin intervention in a particular domain. Underlying this and other instructional strategies is the interventionist's sensitivity and objectivity as an observer of human behavior. To establish the child's developmental level in a certain area, one should assess a child's behavior in relation to a developmental or skill continuum. After the child's level of functioning is determined, the interventionist should behaviorally specify what the child can and cannot do. Once this is accomplished, the training targets may be determined. It is important to define the selected targets operationally, for without a precise definition, members of a staff may disagree about the conditions under which the response should occur or even whether the response has in fact occurred.

During the intervention phase, a variety of instructional strategies should be available. A general underlying strategy is the establishment of contingencies between antecedent events, target responses and consequent events. Most training can be viewed as a triadic equation $A - B - C$ in which A equals the antecedent event, B equals the behavior, and C equals the consequence. The curricula the interventionist works from should specify the arrangement of the environment as well as describing the form of the target response. Consequences can be determined by noting which environmental events in general increase or decrease a particular child's behavior.

Interventionists need to give careful consideration to the training tasks selected to encourage the development of a target objective. An interventionist should not be interested in strict stimulus control; rather, the goal is to help the child acquire general strategies and concepts that can be used across different settings, people, and objects. Learning the label "cup" only for small white cups is not nearly as useful as being able to label all cylindrical containers with handles as cups, regardless of size, color, texture or location.

Selecting tasks that have multiple targets is also important for effective training. In particular, it is often appropriate to superimpose language activities on the training of other skills. In some cases, this might be done simply by placing a few appealing toys on a low table near a child who needs practice both in pulling to a standing position and in labeling objects. The interventionist should be sensitive to the fact that many aspects of a child's natural environment can be used to shape his or her behavior toward the desired target response. Further, tasks should be selected, when possible, that are functionally reinforcing for the child. That is, some aspect of the training activity should be designed to be inherently interesting to the child. For example, on the playground the child is likely to attempt to communicate of his own accord, trying to signal a request to swing or slide. In this instance there is no need to artificially impose the intent to communicate upon the child. Instead, naturally occurring communicative behavior may be effectively shaped toward the target response.

Evaluation of Intervention

Selecting outcome measures that are directly related to the objectives of the intervention efforts is the most useful approach to evaluating a program of intervention. By clearly specifying antecedent and outcome events, an objective evaluation of program outcomes is facilitated. An assessment-linked intervention model should provide the most accurate evaluation of child progress in targeted domains of behavior.

Application of an assessment-linked intervention model requires that a number of criteria be met (Bricker, Seibert, and Scott, in press):

- The evaluation instrument should reflect the curriculum content of the intervention effort.
- The evaluation instrument should have enough flexibility to allow for use with a wide range of handicapped infants.
- The evaluation instrument should have performance criteria that indicate whether the child has a particular skill and whether the skill is functional.
- The evaluation instrument should specify expectancies or rates of acquisition for subpopulations of handicapped children.

Each of these criteria is discussed below in reference to the evaluation of language intervention efforts.

If the target of the intervention program is to enhance a young child's communication skills, then clearly the evaluation instrument needs to focus on progress made toward the acquisition of language behaviors. However, as we have suggested earlier in this chapter, development of language is intertwined in such a way with sensorimotor and affective behavior in the infant as to be functionally inseparable (DeCarie, 1978; Saarni, 1978). This suggests that the focus of intervention as well as evaluation efforts should be directed towards monitoring progress in each of these areas. Considerable progress has been made toward the examining of development in the sensorimotor domain (see for example Uzgiris and Hunt, 1975) but major efforts are still needed to develop useful instrumentation for assessing the development of early language and affective behavior. Each child cannot be unique; the ability to generalize across subpopulations with specified behavioral repertoires and handicapping conditions must be a goal.

If a measurement system is to be used with a variety of handicapped infants and young children, then the evaluation instruments used must have built-in flexibility. And although an instrument must be flexible in its application, standardized administration procedures and response criteria are necessary to meet validity and reliability requirements. Using periodic samples of the child's language may be an appropriate flexible method to monitor progress if the conditions under which the sample is acquired are relatively standard from one sample to the next.

Acquiring specific responses under controlled conditions may be an important first step in the language acquisition process. However, the adaptive use of a response across a variety of settings under different conditions is particularly crucial if a child's communication is to be effective. Evaluation instruments must include mechanisms to determine how functional an acquired language skill is to the child, and whether it can be applied to a variety of situations (White, 1979).

Ultimately the determination of the more effective intervention programs is partly dependent upon the establishment of benchmarks or developmental expectancies for subpopulations of handicapped infants and children. Without the establishment of such benchmarks, one has no idea whether the progress demonstrated by a specific child is on target, given his handicapping conditions; is better than would be expected; or is significantly slower than was predicted. Our language evaluation efforts need to be directed towards the accumulation of information that can be used to construct growth curves for subpopulations of handicapped infants and young children. Such curves might help determine which of the various approaches used in language intervention produce the greatest gains in specific groups of children.

Summary

The steady flow of information generated by psycholinguists, developmental psychologists and educators is providing a rich resource for the development of more effective preverbal communication and early language intervention approaches for handicapped infants. Such information suggests that in planning instruction for communicatively delayed infants, we must broaden our perspectives in at least three directions. First, we need to reckon with the significance of the time period antecedent to the acquisition of referential language, in view of the apparent continuity between preverbal and verbal communication. This emphasis implies that we should extend downward the age for beginning language intervention programming. Second, language development is apparently integrally related to concomitantly developing cognitive and affective systems. Language interventionists need to learn to recognize and to exploit this convergence. Third, the important roles that environmental contexts and complex interactive feedback networks play in the acquisition of child language need to be acknowledged and exploited by language interventionists.

References

Baer, D. M. "The Control of Developmental Process: Why Wait?" In J. R. Nesselroads and J. W. Reese (Eds.), *Life-Span Developmental Psychology: Methodological Issues.* New York: Academic Press, 1973.

Bates, E. "The Emergence of Symbols: Ontogeny and Phylogeny" In W. A. Collins (Ed.), *Children's Language and Communication.* Minnesota Symposia on Child Psychology. Vol. 12. Hillsdale, N.J.: Erlbaum, 1979.

Bricker, D., and Dow, M. "Early Intervention with the Young Severely Handicapped Child." *The Journal of the Association for the Severely Handicapped,* in press.

Bricker, D., Seibert, J., and Casuso, V. "Early Intervention." In J. Hogg and P. Mittler (Eds.), *Advances in Mental Handicap Research.* London: Wiley, 1980.

Bricker, D., Seibert, J., and Scott, K. "Early Intervention: History, Current Status and the Problems of Evaluation." In D. Doleys, T. Vaughn, M. Cantrell (Eds.), *Interdisciplinary Assessment and Treatment of Developmental Problems.* New York: Spectrum, in press.

Brinker, R., and Bricker, D. "Teaching a First Language: Building Complex Structures from Simpler Components." In J. Hogg and P. Mittler (Eds.), *Advances in Mental Handicap Research.* London: Wiley, 1980.

Bruner, J. "From Communication to Language: A Psychological Perspective." *Cognition,* 1975, *3,* 255–287.

DeCarie, T. G. "Affect Development and Cognition in a Piagetian Context." In M. Lewis and L. Rosenblum (Eds.), *The Development of Affect.* New York: Plenum, 1978.

deVilliers, J., and deVilliers, P. *Language Acquisition.* Cambridge, Mass.: Harvard University Press, 1978.

Dore, J. "Holophrases, Speech Acts, and Language Universals." *Journal of Child Language,* 1975, *2,* 1–19.

Guess, D., Sailor, W., and Baer, D. "A Behavioral-Remedial Approach to Language Training for the Severely Handicapped. Reston, Va.: Council for Exceptional Children, 1977.

Hobbs, N. "Classification Options." *Exceptional Children,* 1978, *44,* 494–497.

Mahoney, G. "Ethological Approach to Delayed Language Acquisiton." *American Journal of Mental Deficiency,* 1975, *80* (2), 139–148.

McLean J., and Snyder-McLean, L. *A Transactional Approach to Early Language Training.* Columbus, Ohio: Merrill, 1978.

Nelson, K. "Structure and Strategy in Learning to Talk." *Monographs of the Society for Research in Child Development,* 1973, *38* (1–2), (Serial no. 149).

Piaget, J. "Piaget's Theory." In P. Mussen (Ed.), *Carmichael's Manual of Child Psychology,* Vol I. New York: Wiley, 1970.

Prutting, C. "Process: The Action of Moving Forward Progressively from One Point to Another on the Way to Completion." *Journal of Speech and Hearing Disorders,* 1979, *44* (1), 3–30.

Rosenblatt, D. "Developmental Trends in Infant Play." In B. Tizard and D. Harvey (Eds.), *Biology of Play.* Philadelphia: William Heinemann Medical Books, 1977.

Saarni, C. "Cognitive and Communicative Features of Emotional Experience, or Do You Show What You Think You Feel?" In M. Lewis and L. Rosenblum (Eds.), *The Development of Affect.* New York: Plenum, 1978.

Sugarman, S. "Some Organizational Aspects of Preverbal Communication." In I. Markova (Ed.), *Social Context of Language.* New York: Wiley, 1978.

Tizard, B. "Do Social Relationships Affect Language Development?" In K. Connolly and J. Bruner (Eds.), *The Growth of Competence.* New York: Academic Press, 1974.

Turnbull, A. "Parent-Professional Interactions." In M. Snell (Ed.), *Systematic Instruction of the Moderately and Severely Handicapped.* Columbus, Ohio: Merrill, 1978.

Uzgiris, I., and Hunt, J. McV. *Assessment in Infancy.* Urbana: University of Illinois Press, 1975.

White, O. "Adaptive Performance Assessment." In W. Sailor and L. Brown (Eds.), *Teaching the Severely Handicapped.* Vol. 5. Columbus, Ohio: Special Press, 1979.

Diane Bricker is a professor of special education at the University of Oregon and director of the preschool program for the Center on Human Development.

Laurel Carlson is a doctoral student in special education at the University of Oregon.

Now that some of the basic issues in oral and manual
communication have been resolved, it is projected
that future research will exhibit a pragmatic,
ethological orientation with greater emphasis
on interactions between child and environment.

Language Training with the Young Deaf Child

Julia Maestas y Moores
Donald F. Moores

In considering the needs of children with hearing losses, it has been a common practice to break the hearing impaired population into two groups, deaf and hard of hearing. Each of these groups is further subdivided: the hard of hearing to include mild and moderate hearing losses and the deaf to include severe and profound hearing losses. Those children in the deaf category typically have hearing losses of seventy-five decibels or greater in the better ear with the use of a hearing aid, which means that even under optimal circumstances they cannot process spoken language completely through audition.

The United States Office of Education, Bureau of Education for the Handicapped has estimated that approximately six children per 1,000 have educationally relevant hearing losses (Maestas y Moores and Moores, 1979). Of this number less than one out of six would be considered deaf, or somewhat less than one child in a thousand. In considering early intervention programs, however, children who are identified and receive services tend to have severe and profound hearing losses. Those with less handicapping losses usually are not identified until the school years. The focus of attention in this chapter, then, will be on children who for the most part would have severe to profound hearing losses and who would be considered deaf.

Beginning in the late 1960s, language intervention programs for young deaf children have undergone significant modifications. The establishment and spread of early intervention programs in the public sector in the early 1960s was predicated on a number of assumptions which have been proven false. Perhaps the most persuasive mistaken assumption lay in the belief that techniques and procedures used with primary school-aged deaf children could be easily and effectively extended downward to younger children with only slight modifications (Maestas y Moores and Moores, 1979). There seemed to be little appreciation of the fact that the needs and learning style of a two-year-old are not the same as those of a seven-year-old. A second misguided notion was the preoccupation with what some investigators have characterized as a "denial of deafness" (Meadow, 1968a; Vernon and Koh, 1970). Meadow has been especially concerned with the tendency of professionals to ignore the implications of deafness and concentrate primarily on speech as the predominant concern. By shifting the focus away from deafness and concentrating on only one of its manifestations, many parents have had difficulty in accepting deafness as a lifetime condition and think of it as something transitory which can be cured. Given the present state of our technology, this is not a reasonable hope for the majority of children classified as prelingually deaf.

The third major difficulty may be traced to the residual effects of the oral-manual controversy. At the time of the establishment of significant numbers of early education programs for the hearing impaired in the early 1960s, almost all primary school programs for the deaf—both in day and residential settings—were exclusively oral. These programs did not allow the use of manual communication in the classrooms, under the belief that the use of signs or fingerspelling would detract from the development of speech, English skills and academic achievement. This was influenced by the belief of linguists that a true language could only be spoken (Bloomfield, 1933). As downward extensions of primary/elementary programs, the early intervention programs also were exclusively oral. Change was not effected until the beliefs about the negative effects of manual communication were put to the test and shown to be false. Following that, the situation changed rapidly and by the late 1970s most early intervention programs for the deaf utilized combined oral-manual or total communication (Jordan, Gustason, and Rosen, 1977; Moores, 1979).

Influence of Language Acquisition Theories

Education of the deaf has been subject to the same broad influences as other areas of education. In terms of language acquisition and function, the traditional paradigm has been a behavioral one, with emphasis on the development of vocabulary items and the acquisition of grammatical forms. Concentration was on the mistakes made in speech and writing by deaf subjects, with major attention directed to correct articulation and memorization of grammatical rules. The most widely employed techniques for developing language skills consisted of analytical systems which were taught via drill and exposition (Moores, 1978).

The growing influence of Chomsky (1965, 1968) and his concepts of generative transformational grammar caused some modifications in approaches and led to the development of programs based on a transformational model. The most widely used has been the Rhode Island curriculum (Blackwell, 1978), designed for preschool through secondary grades, which illustrates relationships between propositions which may not be obvious to a naive user of a language. For example, a generative transformational model can show that the following two sentences are similar:

The girl pushed the boy.
The boy was pushed by the girl.

While the following two sentences, although similar on the surface, are not related:

The girl pushed the boy.
The boy pushed the girl.

Such approaches represent attempts to teach correct English grammar to children, and from this standpoint may be considered structural. Although more effective than traditional approaches, they are not designed to incorporate semantic and pragmatic elements of the communication process into the training.

It is clear that future research on the development of language in deaf children will have a broader base, encompassing much more than the sound system and grammar. Rather, the emphasis is shifting toward more functional communication models with a consideration of the interaction of a deaf child within various environmental settings. Rather than attempting to develop specific articulation and grammatical skills, which might not generalize outside of a clinical setting, the thrust will be for the development and assessment of communicative adequacy within naturalistic environments. The area that will receive the greatest attention for the young hearing impaired child will not be the school or clinic, but rather the family and the home. From this base, there will develop strategies for extending relevant research to the community at large, including the schools.

The most important feature that differentiates language training for the young deaf child from that of other children is the fact that the deaf child depends to a great extent on vision for the development of language. In this chapter, research which has influenced present programs will be discussed and described briefly. A discussion of research in progress, with projections for the future, will follow.

Evaluation of Early Intervention Programs for the Deaf

Investigations into the effectiveness of the preschool early intervention programs for the deaf of the early 1960s produced discouraging findings. In essence, the indications were that early intervention programs had no lasting positive effects on speech, grammar, or academic achievement (Craig, 1964; McCroskey, 1968; Phillips, 1963). As discussed above, the programs employed downward extensions of techniques previously utilized with older deaf children.

The lack of positive lasting effects led many programs to experiment with different models, involving a variety of emphases. Moores, Weiss, and Goodwin (1978; in press) conducted a longitudinal evaluation of seven public and residential school programs across the United States over a five-year period. The major findings included:

1. The deaf children functioned in the normal range intellectually when measured by a standardized performance intelligence test (for example, WISC) and by Piagetian measures of conservation, classification and seriation.

2. The deaf children were superior on the Manual Expression subtest of the Illinois Test of Psycholinguistic Abilities to the age norms for hearing children. They scored within the age norms for hearing children on the other four visual-motor subtests.

3. By age seven, the deaf children possessed prereading skills equivalent to hearing children, as measured by a standardized prereading test (for example, Metropolitan Achievement Test). They were below the norms for hearing children in arithmetic.

4. Assessment of parents' attitudes suggested a positive, realistic acceptance of a hearing loss in their children.

5. Strong components of auditory training, speech teaching, and manual communication were incorporated into a program at very early ages. The different components seemed to be complementary and mutually facilitative.

6. The single most effective means of communication was simultaneous use of speech and manual communication (total communication).

7. The most effective programs included cognitive-academic and social components from the beginning. In those programs which were primarily socialization at the beginning, the children never closed the gap in achievement between themselves and children who received early cognitive-academic training.

These results suggest impressive advances in early intervention programs over a ten-year period. The children were of normal intellectual capacity and in some areas were advanced over children with normal hearing. Their academic skills were on target for their age. Parents seemed to be well adjusted. Significant problems, however, still remained. As might be expected with children having severe to profound hearing losses, the speech of most children was difficult to understand. Although the children possessed competent prereading skills, many still had difficulty in comprehending basic English structures, whether presented in print, orally, or through simultaneous oral-manual communication. Complex structures such as negatives and passives tended to be understood as active declarative utterances.

Perhaps the most impressive result was the finding that simultaneous oral-aural-manual communication was effective. Most educators of the deaf — the authors included — had been taught that manual communication impeded the development of speech and language and should be reserved for use only with older children. The data contradict this belief. Human communication need not, indeed should not, be limited to one channel. The high correlations found across different modes of communication suggest that communication is an integrative process that can use more than one channel. The results vindicate the decision that was taken by a majority of the school programs for the deaf in the United States to move toward acceptance of simultaneous oral-manual modes of communication.

Studies of Deaf Children of Deaf Parents

Concurrent with research revealing the relative ineffectiveness of early intervention programs in the 1960s, a spate of research reports appeared indicating that deaf children of deaf parents were superior to deaf children of hearing parents in academic achievement, socialization, and English; with no differences in vocal communication skills (Meadow, 1968b; Quigley and Frisina, 1961; Stevenson, 1964; Stuckless and Birch, 1966). Because a large majority of deaf adults use some form of manual communication, as well as varying degrees of oral communication, the superiority of deaf children of deaf parents was attributed, at least in part, to early use of manual communication. Research in this area, then, provided support for the acceptance of manual communication in the classroom with very young children.

More recent investigations have moved past global academic and linguistic comparisons of children with deaf and hearing parents to investigations of the development of language skills in deaf children of deaf parents in naturalistic settings. McIntyre (1974; 1977) has studied the development of handshapes used by deaf children of deaf parents in communicating from age thirteen to twenty-one months. She found that the acquisition of handshapes follows phonological rules similar to those in the acquisition of phonemes in spoken languages. McIntyre also raised the possibility that early language acquisition in a manual mode may precede vocal production. Her subject used eighty-five signs at thirteen months and was able to employ a question form, utilizing an interrogative marker, at fifteen months. McIntyre (1974, p. 50) concluded:

> The fact that ASL (American Sign Language) is in the visual/ manual modality makes performance available to visual feedback and

the possibility for prompt manual correction. A baby signer can see as well as feel what she is communicating. The muscles required for performance are somewhat larger than those required for vocal languages . . . . At the present it seems safe to assume that deaf children learning their first language are likely to use some very ordinary strategies to acquire a very "ordinary" goal. It is only their language modality which makes the process seem different.

In a similar vein Schlesinger and Meadow (1972) reported that the acquisition of signed vocabulary in deaf children of deaf parents paralleled that of speech in children with normal hearing. Hoffmeister and Moores (1973; 1979), investigating the acquisition of morphology and communicative effectiveness of deaf children of deaf parents, again found the process of acquisition similar to that of spoken language. Audio and video tape evidence shows that four- and five-year-old deaf children can discuss such abstract concepts as death and heaven by means of American Sign Language.

Hoffmeister and Moores have noted some modality differences in the use of manual communication. Visual-motor systems differ from auditory-vocal systems. Visual-motor systems can use three-dimensional space, for example, to convey grammatical and semantic elements or to express unambiguous pronominal relationships that are impossible in spoken languages (see Moores [1978] for a complete treatment of the subject).

Studies of Deaf Children of Hearing Parents

Interactions between hearing parents and their deaf children have received relatively little attention, an unfortunate situation because a large majority of deaf children have hearing parents (Moores, 1980). However, two sets of investigations bear mentioning. The first consists of work conducted by Feldman and Goldin-Meadow (Feldman, 1975; Goldin-Meadow, 1977; Goldin-Meadow and Feldman, 1975) which investigated the language development of five children from one-and-a-half years of age exposed to traditional early intervention procedures with deaf children. (In traditional early intervention procedures, neither the teachers nor the parents were allowed to use any form of manual communication.) By the end of the study, when the children ranged from thirty-two to fifty-four months, two produced no intelligible spoken words and one child produced fewer than five words. The other two children could speak and lipread single words in constrained settings such as pointing to correct items or naming items on flash cards. There was no transfer observed of speech and lipreading to general activities of daily living.

The lack of development in oral skills led the children to develop gestural systems for the purpose of symbolic communication. They invented gestures to refer to lexical items and then combined the gestures into two-unit phrases. Goldin-Meadow and Feldman (1975) concluded that a deaf child not exposed to a gesture system may invent one. These investigators reported that the children do not merely imitate the inadvertent gestures of parents but they appear to develop a language-like system without benefit of a conventional linguistic model.

Whether deaf children do invent complex linguistic systems is a debatable issue and depends to a large extent on one's definition of "linguistic." It seems clear, however, that human beings have an urge to communicate. If they are blocked in one area, they will use whatever means at their disposal to compensate.

Crandell (1974) studied fourteen deaf children of hearing parents and six deaf children of deaf parents from three to seven years of age and analyzed the development of their language skills. In this study, the hearing parents also used sign language beginning as early as twenty-four months. She reported that those children whose mothers tended to sign in grammatically correct English also were able to sign in grammatically correct English by seven years of age. The need for intensive parental instruction was stressed. Crandell also reported that early auditory stimulation, even for profoundly hearing impaired children, was useful in learning signs. In other words, multifaceted imput was preferable to a unimodal training strategy. Crandell concluded that there was a reinforcing relationship between the use of speech and the use of sign language, a conclusion similar to that reached by Moores, Weiss, and Goodwin (1978) in their evaluation of early intervention programs.

Current Trends

As mentioned in the first section of the chapter, research is being conducted to study communication abilities across a range of environments. Just as research with children with normal hearing increasingly concentrates on what might have been considered prelinguistic behavior, it is inevitable that those concerned with the development of deaf children will turn toward the study of younger children. Condon (1976) refers to an "interactional synchrony" between mother and child which begins in the first day of life and which may exist even *in utero*. He speculates that such synchrony may reflect the existence of a basic short-term latency phase in the human responding process. If such is the case, it is necessary to identify essential elements for the parent-child interaction in order to facilitate the development of deaf children.

A related area of interest must be parental input to children at different levels of development. For example, it has been found that parents use exaggerated intonation, lengthen vowels, and are repetitious with children during the first year of life (Blount and Kempton, 1976). Adult speech to children tends to consist of shorter, simpler, and more redundant utterances (Broen, 1972). It has even been demonstrated that parents of Down's Syndrome children appropriately modify their speech to their handicapped children as a function of the child's level of linguistic development (Rondal, 1978). The same processes may occur with parents of deaf children: however, research is needed to document this assumption.

Givens (1978), noting that infants participate in complex forms of interaction during the first year of life, has suggested that early gestures may be the basis for later signs. He has called for establishment of ethologically oriented research in naturalistic environments. This research would incorporate such behaviors as touching, smiling, vocalizing, and sucking in consideration of the development of communication.

Research in language acquisition in general is taking on a much broader perspective with concern for the development of pragmatic functions of language in addition to the areas of phonology, grammar, and semantics. Many investigators are concentrating on the semantic bases of language and have emphasized the importance of pragmatics in the acquisition and use of language. Despite the influence of Chomsky, the field of developmental psycholinguistics increasingly embraces performance and not competency models of language. At the same time, by assigning an important role to semantics, the orientation is much broader than Skinnerian Behaviorism. Another notable shift that has occurred is related to the age-old nature-nurture controversy. The work of Chomsky wrenched most American scientists concerned with language acquisition away from a preoccupation with environmental factors. The pendulum swung from a position of predominant attention on the environment to one of predominant attention on innate abilities of human beings to acquire language. Under this paradigm, theories of learning and psychological techniques involving such principles as reinforcement, redundancy, and contiguity were dismissed as irrelevant for language acquisition (Chomsky, 1959; McNeill, 1966).

The predominant approach at present is clearly interactional, with attention devoted to the reciprocal nature of the interaction between the developing child and the environment. There seems to be an integration of elements of behaviorism and of Chomsky's nativist orientation. This integration is not the welding of two disparate philosophies; rather it appears to be a new paradigm which synthesizes elements of both theoretical approaches to produce a broader perspective.

We believe that future research on language acquisition will be characterized by an ethological orientation with an emphasis on child-environment interactions. Much of the work will be with children under the age of twelve months and will examine behaviors which have until recently been considered prelinguistic.

Such an orientation presents a number of exciting opportunities and challenges. In the case of deaf children, it presents some formidable methodological problems. The major difficulty is that severe hearing loss usually is not diagnosed in the first year of life. Once diagnosed, there is frequent uncertainty over the extent of the loss and the potential for utilization of residual hearing.

Another complication which has not received adequate attention is the emotional state of the family (Moores, 1978). The majority of parents of deaf children have normal hearing and have little understanding of the implications of a severe hearing loss. The process of diagnosis itself frequently is drawn out and emotionally draining. Recrimination and blame are not uncommon for parents. Most parents go through a period of confusion and grief at a time when the child needs immediate attention. The process of hearing is a mystery to most parents; the fitting and monitoring of a hearing aid for their young child is threatening; and the use of manual communication foreign to them.

Obviously, the needs of the parents as they work through feelings of grief, guilt and helplessness must be sensitively balanced against the needs of the child. Technical competence in manual communication and the use of hearing aids is not enough.

One way to help parents meet the needs of their children would be to analyze the behavior of deaf parents who apparently are able to raise both deaf and hearing children in such a way that they acquire proficiency in communication skills. The linguistic, academic and social superiority of deaf children of deaf parents over deaf children of hearing parents has been extensively documented. In addition, hearing children of deaf parents grow up and achieve normal levels of proficiency in spoken English. There is strong reason to believe, then, that deaf parents provide appropriate environments for the development of linguistic skills in children, whether deaf or hearing. The linguistic superiority of deaf children of deaf parents may be explained in large part by the use of early manual communication. The easier acceptance of deafness by deaf parents without the trauma which accompanies it for most hearing parents also probably plays an important part. In addition to manual communication and a greater willingness to accept deafness, deaf parents utilize procedures and techniques that hearing parents do not use in interacting with young hearing impaired children. Such techniques obviously are not necessary for those children with normal hearing, who generally acquire English proficiency regardless of parental hearing status. However, if effective techniques and procedures could be identified, they might prove of inestimable benefit for hearing parents of deaf children.

Although the majority of children of deaf parents have normal hearing, the chances of deafness are higher than in the general population. Since the largest etiological category of deafness is "cause unknown" many parents do not know if the source of their own deafness was genetic in nature. Even when the etiology for both parents can be traced to recessive hereditary deafness, children could have normal hearing because of the varieties of recessive deafness (Moores, 1978). An interesting outcome has been that little research on the development of children of deaf parents has been conducted before the second year of life, primarily because the identification of a hearing loss usually is not made until after that time.

Deaf parents, then, typically interact with a child during the first year of life in an atmosphere of uncertainty regarding the child's hearing status. An analysis of the parental environment provided by deaf adults during the first months of a child's life should provide insights into the establishing of necessary and sufficient conditions to allow children to achieve communicative proficiency in a relaxed and natural manner.

An Ethnograpic Pilot Study

Maestas y Moores (1979) is investigating the interactions between deaf parents and children from birth to eighteen months of age. Subjects consist of nine families with profoundly deaf parents and children one-and-a-half years of age. Mother and child were filmed in the home once a month under natural conditions. Although the analysis is not complete, a number of characteristics of the parent-child interaction have been identified which are of interest.

Signing on Child's Body. Most signs used by adults are made within a space in front of the body. Parents have been observed to make signs using the child's body as a reference point. For example, one mother made the sign "cute" on the baby's chin rather than her own to indicate that he was cute. Other signs such as "hungry," "love," "your," "wash," "sleep," and so on, have also been made on the baby's body. The frequent use of the child's body suggests that for the young child with deaf parents language involves a large amount of physical contact.

Modeling. Using the term to refer to physically guiding a child through a sign or series of signs, it can be seen that the sense of touch again plays an important role. This was observed as early as one day, with a child's hand held to wave bye-bye. By thirteen weeks one child was led through signs for pat-a-cake. Other parents shape children's hands for fingerspelling by three months and shape signs such as squirrel and turtle. A mother manually guided her child through the sequence "I love my mommy" at three months. Signing and nursery rhymes involving body contact between mother and child are freqent. McIntyre's (1974; 1977) previously noted comments concerning the early acquisition of signs attributable to the nature of a visual-motor system seems to be supported by these observations.

Tactile Kinesthetic Information. Mothers sign to children even when their eyes are closed. For example, when feeding in the mother's arms, the mother might sign using the arm that is holding the baby. She might also sign to other children or adults while holding the baby.

Signing Style. Because signing space is more constricted with babies than for other individuals, the signs tend to be smaller and close to the baby's face. There is also a relatively large number of one hand signs, especially when holding, feeding or bathing the baby.

Modality. Neither parents nor children are limited to one modality. All of the following modes are common and have been observed with all children: signs, fingerspelling, or voice alone; signs or fingerspelling with voice;

signs or fingerspelling without voice but with lip movement; lip movement alone. Although the clarity of speech of the parents varied, all utilized speech to some extent. The most common mode for all parents was simultaneous speech and signs.

Fingerspelling. There has been considerable debate among educators of the deaf over the ability of young children to process fingerspelling, with the majority believing it should not be used with young children. This position has been challenged by Russian reports of success with children as young as two years of age (Moores, 1978). Parents in the pilot study fingerspelled as well as signed to children at early ages, with one parent signing to a one-day-old baby "your name is " and then spelling "Arturo."

Cross-Modal Communication. Mother and child may operate comfortably in different modes. For example, one mother speechread her eleven-month-old vocalizing "dadadadada" and responded in sign "Daddy not home now." At the same age, the child responded to the mother's signs "Good" and "No" with what the investigator interpreted as a vocal appreciation of the words. Children and parents seem comfortable moving across modes; the process of communication is not unitary. Whether a message is spoken or signed appears to have relatively less importance than the purpose it serves.

Orienting Strategies. Unlike dealing with adults, in which attempts to attract attention involve moving the hands or arms, the attention of children frequently is obtained by physical contact. For very young children, the mother will take the child's face in her hands and gently move it to face her while she is signing. At older ages this is accomplished by moving the face with a hand or two fingers under the chin. For children over six months, the parent may tap the child's shoulder or leg, or place her hand on the child's body to gain his or her attention.

Conclusion

Significant progress has been made in recent years in understanding the process of language acquisition and in applying this understanding to facilitate the linguistic development of deaf children. For the future the most potentially fruitful efforts would appear to be related to pragmatics and to semantic bases of language. It is projected that research will be conducted to a greater extent under an ethological model, concentrating on child/environment interactions, and will extend downward to include the first year of life.

Both in the classroom and in less formal settings the trend seems to be toward a multisensory model. Auditory training, manual communication, and speech training are being introduced at early ages and are used in coordination with one another. Programs are finally beginning to look at the needs of the child and of members of the entire family as highly interrelated. There is less tendency to think in terms of the communication problems of the child in isolation. Rather the child is conceived of as a social being with complex patterns of active reactions and interactions relative to individuals in his environment.

References

Blackwell, P. *Sentences and Other Systems.* Washington, D. C.: A. G. Bell Association, 1978.

Bloomfield, L. *Language.* New York: Holt, Rinehart and Winston, 1933.

Blount, B., and Kempton, W. "Child Language Socialization: Parental Speech and Interactional Strategies." *Sign Language Studies,* 1976, *12,* 251–277.

Broen, P. "The Verbal Environment of the Language Learning Child." *American Speech and Hearing Association Monographs,* 1972.

Chomsky, N. "Review of Skinner's Verbal Behavior." *Language,* 1959, *35,* 26–58.

Chomsky, N. *Aspects of the Theory of Syntax.* Cambridge, Mass.: M.I.T. Press, 1965.

Chomsky, N. *Language and Mind.* New York: Harcourt Brace Jovanovich, 1968.

Condon, W. "An Analysis of Behavioral Organization." *Sign Language Studies,* 1976, *13,* 285–318.

Craig, W. "Effects of Preschool Training on the Development of Reading and Lipreading Skills of Deaf Children." *American Annals of the Deaf,* 1964, *109,* 280–296.

Crandell, K. "A Study of the Production of Chers and Related Sign Language Aspects by Deaf Children Between the Ages of Three and Seven Years." Unpublished doctoral dissertation, Northwestern University, 1974.

Feldman, H. "The Development of a Lexicon by Deaf Children of Hearing Parents." Unpublished doctoral dissertation, University of Pennsylvania, 1975.

Givens, D. "Social Expressivity During the First Year of Life." *Sign Language Studies,* 1978, *20,* 251–274.

Goldin-Meadow, S. "Structure in a Manual Communication System Developed Without a Conventional Language Model." Unpublished doctoral dissertation, University of Chicago, 1977.

Goldin-Meadow, S., and Feldman, H. "The Creation of a Communication System: A Study of Deaf Children of Hearing Parents." *Sign Language Studies,* 1975, *8,* 225–234.

Hoffmeister, R., and Moores, D. *The Acquisition of Specific Reference in a Deaf Child of Deaf Parents.* Research Report No. 33. Minneapolis: Research and Development Center in Education of Handicapped Children, University of Minnesota, 1973.

Hoffmeister, R., and Moores, D. "Predicting the Extent of the Abstract Abilities of Deaf Children." Paper presented at American Instructors of the Deaf National Convention, Austin, Texas, June, 1979.

Jordan, I., Gustason, G., and Rosen, R. "Current Communication Trends in Programs for the Deaf." *American Annals of the Deaf,* 1977, *121,* 521–531.

McCroskey, R. "Final Progress Report of Four-Year Home Training Program." Paper read at A. G. Bell National Convention, San Francisco, June 1968.

McIntyre, M. "A Modified Model for the Description of Language Acquisitin in a Deaf Child." Unpublished master's thesis, California State University, Northridge, 1974.

McIntyre, M. "The Acquisition of American Sign Language Hand Configurations." *Sign Language Studies,* 1977, *16,* 244–266.

McNeill, D. "Developmental Psycholinguistics," In F. Smith and G. Miller (Eds.), *The Genesis of Language.* Cambridge, Mass,: M.I.T. Press, 1966.

Maestas y Moores, J. "Communication Patterns Between Deaf Parents and Very Young Children: A Touching Experience." Paper presented at New Jersey Speech and Hearing Association Annual Meeting, Somerset, New Jersey, May 20, 1979.

Maestas y Moores, J., and Moores, D. "Educational Alternatives for the Hearing Impaired." In M. Nerbonne and R. Schow (Eds.), *Aural Rehabilitation.* Baltimore: University Park Press, 1979.

Meadow, K. "Parental Response to the Medical Ambiguities of Deafness." *Journal of Health and Social Behavior,* 1968a. *9,* 299–309.

Meadow, K. "Early Manual Communication in Relation to the Deaf Child's Intellectual, Social, and Communicative Functioning." *American Annals of the Deaf,* 1968b, *113,* 29–41.

Moores, D. *Educating the Deaf: Psychology, Principles and Practices.* Boston: Houghton Mifflin, 1978.

Moores, D. "Hearing Impairments." In S. Lilly (Ed.), *Children with Exceptional Needs.* New York: Holt, Rinehart and Winston, 1979.

Moores, D. "Auditory Dysfunctions." In R. Smith and J. Neisworth (Eds.), *The Exceptional Child.* New York: McGraw Hill, 1980.

Moores, D., Weiss, K., and Goodwin, M. "Early Education Programs for Hearing Impaired Children: Major Findings." *American Annals of the Deaf,* 1978, *123,* 925–936.

Moores, D., Weiss, K., and Goodwin, M. "Early Intervention Programs for Hearing Impaired Children." *American Speech and Hearing Association Monographs,* in press.

Phillips, D. "Influence of Preschool Training on Language Arts, Arithmetic Concepts, and Socialization of Young Deaf Children." Unpublished doctoral dissertation, Teachers College, Columbia University, 1963.

Quigley, S., and Frisina, D. *Institutionalization and Psycho-Educational Development of Deaf Children.* Washington, D.C.: Council for Exceptional Children, 1961.

Rondal, J. "Maternal Speech to Normal and Down's Syndrome Children Matched for Mean Length of Utterance." *American Journal of Mental Deficiency Monograph,* 1978, *3,* 193–265.

Schlesinger, H., and Meadow, K. "The Development of Maturity in Deaf Children.' *Exceptional Children,* 1972, *39,* 461–467.

Stevenson, E. "A Study of the Educational Achievement of Deaf Children of Deaf Parents." *California News,* 1964, *80,* 143.

Stuckless, E., and Birch, J. "The Influence of Early Manual Communication on the Linguistic Development of Deaf Children," *American Annals of the Deaf,* 1966, *111,* 499–504.

Vernon, M., and Koh, S. "Effects of Manual Communication on Deaf Children's Educational Achievement, Linguistic Competence, Oral Skills, and Psychological Development." *American Annals of the Deaf,* 1970, *15,* 527–536.

Julia Maestas y Moores is a doctoral candidate in educational psychology at the University of Minnesota

Donald F. Moores is professor of special education and communicative disorders and head of the division of special education and communication disorders at The Pennsylvania State Universiy.

The nonspeech child should be provided with an augmentative system for communication. Factors to be considered in the selection of such a system are discussed.

Communication Systems for Nonspeech Children

David E. Yoder

The problem discussed in this chapter is the one faced by teachers, clinicians, parents, rehabilitation counselors and others trying to develop an effective means of communication for children who are nonspeaking. The term nonspeech child as used here refers to those individuals for whom speech is not *now* a functional means of meeting their communication needs. This does not mean the child has no speech or vocalization abilities, nor does it mean that the child may not develop fully functional speech in the future. There is evidence that augmentative communication aids and systems do promote speech, both developmentally and for functional use. We are referring to nonspeech children as those who are at present severely handicapped in communicating because they are unable to fulfill their communication needs with their limited or nonexistent speech abilities. In the United States, there are an estimated 1,225,000 children who are nonspeaking, or severely speech impaired as a result of a neurological, physical, or psychological disability. Children whose nonspeech behavior results primarily from hearing impairment and/or deafness are not included in this discussion (see Maestas y Moores, and Moores this volume).

The term nonspeech children, as used in this chapter, groups together completely nonvocal, nonoral, nonvocal/nonoral, nonspeech with potential for later development of speech, and the partially speaking (severe intelligibility problems). This is done for the following reasons: All of these children have the same problem—a nonfunctional communication system; they all need a means to augment their present way of communicating in order to compensate for partial or complete inadequacies in their oral communication system; and they all have similar communication needs. With respect to a nonfunctional communication system, this is viewed primarily as an ineffective means to express ideas, thoughts, and needs. Because of severe speech-motor problems (both congenital and acquired), the child is not able to formulate the sounds, words and phrases in an intelligible manner. On the other hand, a number of neurologically, cognitively, and emotionally impaired children may not have acquired the receptive, comprehension and/or expressive skills for effective speech communication. In the latter case, finding an effective communication system means finding a system through which the child acquires comprehension as well as expressive skills.

All nonspeech children need an augmentative means of communicating and interacting. The emphasis here is on the concept of *augmentation*. When speech is not currently useful as the major means of communication, we look for supplementary techniques and systems to enhance and facilitate communication by complementation of whatever vocal/oral skills the individual possesses. Harris and Vanderheiden (1979) suggest that use of augmentative techniques supplement speech in partially vocal-speaking persons, and facilitates the development of language and communication in persons who can not yet speak, but may eventually develop functional speech. It is suggested that if augmentative communication techniques and systems are implemented early, delayed development in the motor control necessary for speech and fine motor movement need not have severe delaying effects upon the development of language and social skills. A necessary point to make here is augmentative systems and techniques are not to be viewed as alternatives for speech. The term *alternative system* rather than "augmentative" system reflects the notion of failure or defeat for the nonspeech child ("you have failed at speaking, and so we will replace speech"). This certainly reduces the importance of speech in partially vocal and speaking individuals, and further suggests that from now on speech is ruled out. Only when there is incontrovertible evidence that the child will not ever be able to use speech should we think of the notion of replacing speech with an aid or device. If possible, speech therapy should continue as part of the child's habilitation program, even though an augmentative system has been adopted.

Regardless of the living environment, educational setting and eventual vocational placement, there are communication demands which are quite similar with respect to everyday functions. Whether we are persons who use or are unable to use speech has little to do with the personal demands which are present for communication and interaction. Consequently, having an augmentative aid available allows for the use of the system when speech skills are inadequate or when the unfamiliarity of those with whom nonspeech children interact prevents communication via speech.

Nonspeech Variables to Consider

We have discussed the fact that nonspeaking children vary in their speech and communication abilities, but there are additional ways in which they will differ. These variables are interactive with the speech-communication problem the person exhibits. For that reason, when working to develop effective communication systems for the widely varying population, it is necessary to bring together an interdisciplinary team to determine the best solutions and approaches.

Age. Communication needs will differ with age, and there will be an interaction of age with all the variables which follow. The point to keep in mind is that communication and language development are directly related to motor, cognitive and sensory developmental phenomena. The gaps which may appear between and among these behaviors are important to note, both for selecting an appropriate augmentative system and aid and for predicting how it will be used by the child.

Cognitive Ability. Many nonspeaking children may experience cognitive deficits in conjunction with motor and social skill development problems. These deficits may range from mild to severe mental retardation. The child with a mild or moderate cognitive delay may only be slow in acquiring and using the augmentative system selected. However, the child with severe cognitive deficits in addition to severe motoric handicaps will require special consideration, and possibly a combination of techniques and approaches in the development and use of a communication system. Chapman and Miller (1979) and Reichle and Yoder (in press) suggest that augmentative communication systems will not be successfully acquired or used until the child has reached the sensorimotor stage of V and VI.

Motor Ability. The extent of the physical and motor problem manifested by the child can have definite consequences on communication and cognitive development. Primary reduction or inconsistent ability to interact with and explore the environment through play or vocalizations present a number of complications in developing communication and interaction skills in general, and also in learning to use an augmentative system. Impairment of motor coordination handicaps the child's ability to explore, manipulate and experience objects, persons and events in the environment. Piaget (1964) has postulated that throughout the sensorimotor period (0 to 21 months) motoric interaction and object manipulation are important for the development of symbolic representation and related cognitive skills which are prerequisite to the development and use of language. We also find that reduced and inconsistent ability to play and interact with primary caregivers, peers, and others through "usual" motor patterning and movements (facial, vocal, and verbal imitations) adversely effects the development of cognitive and linguistic skills (Yarrow and others, 1975). Nonspeaking children with severe physical handicaps are frequently unable to stimulate positive affect from caregivers in their environment. Social interaction is frequently decreased due to the spastic or athetoid movements, persistence of infantile reflex patterns, involuntary facial grimaces, lack of consistent smiling responses, and the necessity for continual supportive care in daily living skills. Motor-related handicaps do result in social, interactional, motivational, and communicative handicaps. In addition, most augmentative communication systems are basically operated through motor movements of one sort or another; therefore, it is of importance whether the child has the motor coordination to point to objects and symbols, or has motor posture movement problems that make the use of any type of communication device difficult.

Visual Ability. The environment is explored not only by means of motor interaction, but visually as well. During the first few months of life, children engage in visual tracking, localizing, and nonspeech communicative acts of "line of regard" (Reichle and Yoder, 1979). Essentially, children are engaging in "eye pointing" which is intended to direct the attention or actions of other persons in the environment to specific objects, events, and actions of interest to the child. For many motor-handicapped children who do not have the ability to grasp, reach, and point for and to objects, the use of the eyes for carrying out such activities becomes extremely important. The use of the eyes for pointing to objects and symbols on augmentative aids may be the most efficient mode for communication. Bruner (1975) has pointed out the importance of vision as it relates to the development of cognitive skills as well as for social and communication purposes.

Communication Ability. Frequently we become so engrossed in the speech motor mechanism as the primary cause of speech and communication problems that we fail to look at other modes of interaction which may be appropriate for communication. We must look beyond the motoric barriers to communication development. For example, the child may experience an inability to express sounds of happiness, sadness, pain/discomfort and other affective feelings. There may be the inability to express ideas, requests, and demands through speech, and as a result of the severe speech mechanism disorder that disallows such behavior, the child is thought to be noncommunicative or alinguistic. Our insensitivity to the nonspeaking child's nonspeech communication, in relation to any type of communication other than speech, may inhibit the development of communication and interaction in the young child. This attitude, we have found, also kills most motivation to communicate, regardless of the system or aid available.

The Environment. Yarrow and others (1975) suggest that early cognitive and communication development can be significantly related to the level of social stimulation, intensity of expression of positive affect, active kinesthetic stimulation, and variety in the inanimate environment. This suggests that we must be attentive to issues from the first few months of life with the severely handicapped child, to assist in providing experiences that facilitate cognitive and communicative behavior. In the case where motor behaviors interfere with routine care, we find that caregivers may react negatively to the child. For example, feeding, bathing, dressing, and playing with the infant and young child is usually a warm and rewarding situation for both the child and caregiver. However, frustration and tension may replace these feelings when the caregiver is uncomfortable in dealing with the physically handicapped, nonspeaking child's erratic, involuntary, and spastic movements. Consequently, children may spend considerable time in physical environments which change infrequently, and in social environments which do not provide much touching, holding, hugging, or other physical contact. We must be continually aware of the living situation and the educational environment, as well as the community of prospective interacters with the nonspeaking child. Not only are we concerned about the situation for acquiring the appropriate communication skills, but we must be equally cognizant of the interaction which can take place with the nonspeaking child once an augmentative system has been selected.

The Team that Assists in Decision Making

Looking at this list of variables brings us immediately to the issue of who is most appropriate to make decisions for the nonspeaking child in regard to augmentative systems or aids best suited to his or her abilities and needs. It becomes obvious when looking at this list of variables that no professional discipline is sufficiently knowledgeable to make such a decision alone. Consequently, people from a variety of disciplines, working as a team, are needed. Because of the nature of the communication problem, the professional who understands language and communication development, speech-motor disorders, and has experience in speech, language and communication programming should head the interdisciplinary team. While it may be the major responsibility of this person to coordinate the information necessary to make the communication system and aid choice, it is not and cannot be the full responsibility of this person to make the decisions.

The professional team should have input from the parents, since there is probably no one who knows the child better than the primary caregivers (parents). It is therefore extremely important to include them in the decision-making process. If the child is in an educational placement, then the teacher or an educational consultant should have major input into the selection of the augmentative system. Because of the motor and physical problems which the child has, and may continue to have, it is necessary to have consultants who know motor behavior well. Where possible, both an occupational therapist and physical therapist should be included on the team.

Today there are persons who are specially trained to deal with the problems of positioning and prosthesis fitting. If such an individual is available, then, it may be of importance to seek that person's advice relative to positioning the potential aid user, and to arrive at the best means of accessing the communication board or device. Along with the growth of information regarding communication devices has come a group of persons who are specialists in this area. Most people who function in this capacity are speech and language clinicians. The point to be made is that before any aid, device, or system is selected, the potential user must be evaluated in light of what aids and systems are available for that person. There is no one communication system or device which will meet the needs of all children who are nonspeaking. There are a number of systems and devices, and from this variety a best fit can be made. Selecting the most appropriate system requires much information and thought on the part of the team who studies the nonspeech child. The most neglected person in this entire selection process is usually the user of the communication system. Whenever possible, the child should be included in the selection process. We take from the child cognitive, motor, speech, communication, and other behavioral data, but we usually fail to seek their advice or wish when choosing the system or device. In many cases, they may not be able to make a choice, or so it may seem to us, but whenever possible, they must have a vote on what is going to eventually be their communication system with the world. Each team member must come to this task with an appreciation of the essential expertise of each other member, including the potential user, for without their collective contributions, the foundations for successful augmentative communication will not be laid.

The Physical Mechanism for Augmentative Communication

Since the nonspeaking children comprising the subject of this chapter do not have the oral speech-motor mechanism available for speech, or may suffer from other neurological or emotional disorders which preclude acquiring and using speech as a means of communication, it is necessary to develop a means that will allow the child to communicate. There are a number of techniques that have been developed to allow any child, no matter how severely handicapped, to effectively indicate communication messages to receivers. (A complete review of techniques may be found in Vanderheiden and Harris-Vanderheiden, 1976; Vanderheiden and Grilley, 1975; and Vanderheiden, 1978.)

Techniques and aids have been developed to provide the nonspeech child with a means of interacting with others. These techniques and aids vary from simple manual communication boards, which the child uses by pointing to the message elements (such as pictures) needed, to advanced portable electronic communication aids that are capable of translating the erratic pointing movements of the severely handicapped cerebral palsy individual into a printed message and computerized speech. The number of commercially available communication aids has increased dramatically in the last few years and with future advances in engineering and technology will continue to increase. With the array of communication techniques and aids presently being marketed, the selection process for professionals and consumers has become complex.

Each technique developed for the nonspeech child has advantages and disadvantages, and is more applicable to some types of disabilities than to others. Some of the techniques require minimal motor control, while others use refined movements. Vanderheiden and Harris-Vanderheiden (1976) suggest that the greater the number and complexity of a child's controlled movements, the faster his speed of communication can be. To achieve optimal speed, however, a child must be matched with the technique that best utilizes his particular type and degree of motor control.

As mentioned earlier, the child's age and cognitive abilities will influence language and communication development and use. They will likewise influence the applicability of a technique or aid. Both the complexity of the technique and the types of symbols that can be used with the technique or aid must be examined in relation to the child's present and best estimate of future capabilities. A technique that requires the use of a complex code, or an aid that requires the user to spell, may be inappropriate for a child who has not reached the appropriate stage of cognitive development.

There is no "one system" for a particular child, but there is usually a technique or aid that is most effective, given a careful evaluation of the environmental demands, communication needs, cognitive abilities, and motor skills of the child. As the child develops, the environment, the communication needs, and cognitive and motor abilities will change. To meet these changes, the communication system—along with the techniques and aids—will need to be reevaluated and revised as necessary. Augmentative communication systems must be dynamic, just as speech and language are dynamic for speaking persons. For this reason, the selection of a technique and system that is functionally flexible is desirable.

Basic Techniques for Augmentative Communication

Vanderheiden and Harris-Vanderheiden (1976) suggest that all the techniques available for providing nonspeech children a means of communication interaction fall into three basic approaches. (For a full discussion of these approaches, please refer to the above reference, as well as Vanderheiden and Grilley, 1975; and Vanderheiden, 1978.)

Communication which relies on a direct selection technique is one in which the user indicates directly the desired message elements. This is usually accomplished by the person pointing to the desired object, symbol, or word. Simple communication boards can be put together without great expense for use by the nonspeech child (Vicker, 1974). On the other hand, very sophisticated and independent direct selection aids are available.

A major advantage of the direct selection approach is its straightforward nature, which involves no learning of the technique required except pointing. Direct selection aids have been successful with low-functioning children, and the potential speed of communicating with this approach is limited only by the pointing speed of the child. In putting together such an aid for a child, one must be mindful of the child's range of motion. This is true both for positioning the aid for best access, as well as for the arrangement of the vocabulary display on the aid, whether it is pictures, symbolics, or words. Direct selection aids are useful for ambulatory children, as well as those confined to a wheelchair or walker. Putting together a display for the ambulatory child may require innovative and creative ideas on the part of the clinician, teacher, or parent. But in each case the aid must be developed to best fit the child's abilities and needs. In one case, a small apron-like communication aid was fitted for a young ambulatory girl, but the same type of arrangement met with resistance from a boy of similar age and functioning level. For him, a display was bonded between two pieces of plastic, rolled up and carried in a toy gun holster, belted around his waist.

The direct selection approach provides a comparatively efficient, fast, and simple means of communication for the child who has the motor control for pointing and an adequate range of motion. A note to keep in mind is that when we talk of range of motion, it need not be restricted to range of the arms and hands. Many children use pointing sticks attached to a harness around the head, or a pointing stick held between the teeth. Pointing and direct selection may also be done with the eyes.

A second approach is that of scanning. In this approach the user responds with a prearranged signal or switch to the desired message elements, as they appear in a predetermined sequence. The simplest and probably most-used example of the scanning approach is the yes/no "twenty questions" guessing game. Here we have established some prearranged yes/no signal, which may be a head nod, diverted eye gaze, movement of hand, or any other detectable sign of which the child is capable. The person interacting with the child presents the child with question choices one at a time, and the child signals "yes" when the sender reaches the desired question or message element. In a classroom situation, the teacher may point individually to stimuli on a communication board. Again, the child responds to the sender with some signal when the person points to the desired element.

Today there are a number of automatic sequencing aids available, ranging from simple to complex. The switching devices available are such that no matter how severely physically handicapped the child, he or she can be taught to effectively indicate communication elements on a scanning device. Since they are simple to operate, even low-functioning children can use them. The major disadvantage of the scanning approach is its relative slowness. On the other hand, technology has provided individual speed control for the user, and new switching devices do allow for scanning in a more efficient manner than was possible a year ago. Technology will probably allow for more effective and efficient scanning aids in the future.

The third approach is that of encoding. Mutual code systems are the major component here. The message being communicated is indicated by multiple signals from the child in a pattern that must be known or accessible to the receiver of the message. The Morse code is an example of such a system. A message can be sent by pointing to a series of numbers, colors, or letters arranged on a display corresponding with a vocabulary list or board elsewhere. For example, a severely handicapped young man, who spent most of his day in a semireclining position on an ortho-cart, had a plexiglass board suspended above him on which was a series of numbers corresponding to a vocabulary list posted on the wall of the classroom. By pointing to a single number, or combination of numbers, he was able to indicate the word, words, or phrases listed on the vocabulary list which he wanted to communicate. Encoding techniques provide a fast means of communication, and a means of accessing large vocabularies with limited movement. However, the encoding technique requires relatively complex cognitive skills and, in many cases, greater physical control than scanning aids. Some of the newer encoding aids are very sophisticated, and interface with automated speech.

Placing all communication approaches under these three categories is somewhat simplistic. The different approaches are frequently combined, to take advantage of the individual assets of each approach. Such combinations can be better and more efficiently fitted to the individual needs of children. Consequently, it is possible to combine the technology of the scanning aid with the construct of the encoding technique and have a scan-encode system. This is being incorporated in a number of different communication aids presently being marketed (Vanderheiden, 1978).

Introducing the Child to the Augmentative Communication Device

Regardless of the augmentative communication technique chosen, it should be introduced to the child through play and interactive activities. Harris and Vanderheiden (1979) suggest that severely handicapped children who may not have pointing skills may be able to voluntarily control a light which scans across a matrix by utilizing a controllable gross motor movement, such as moving the head, arm, foot, leg, or knee. This experience, they say, can eventually be transferred for use in communication by having the child activate and stop a light which scans through a vocabulary matrix of pictures, symbols or words. The suggestion here is that the child be given experiences in nonlinguistic settings which allow for certain interactions and control of the environment; these experiences can later be used for communication purposes. The child could be allowed to activate toys, radios, televisions, and other environmental objects through starting and stopping the selector light on various squares of a matrix. In other words, the child is playing with, interacting with, and controlling aspects of the environment with the same technique through which communicative intent will later be expressed. While motivation to communicate by means of an augmentative system is a problem in many cases, early experience with environmental control can lead to such activities becoming reinforcing and pleasurable. These experiences should lead naturally to using the "fun" technique for more complex communication activities, much in the way early vocal and motor behavior of nonhandicapped children leads into speech behavior.

Augmentative Symbol Systems

Now that we have discussed techniques by which communication interaction can take place between two persons — one basically a nonspeaker — it is appropriate to examine various symbol systems which might be used with the techniques and aids. The symbol system chosen for the child must provide a means for representing thoughts in a form that can be physically transmitted or presented to those with whom the child will be interacting.

For young children, as well as those functioning cognitively at sensorimotor stage V and VI, the selection and development of a symbol system and vocabulary is more important to communication effectiveness than is the specific augmentative aid or technique. The symbol system and individual vocabulary selected will mark the success of the communication system for the child. Just as there is no one technique or aid for a child, there is no one symbol system or vocabulary for a child. What may have been determined as the most effective symbol system in the initial evaluation period may change over time because of developmental and environmental changes. The selection process is therefore to be viewed as continuous and dynamic.

It is also important to view the selection and development of symbol system strategies in light of the multiple environments with which the child may interact. For example, what might be best suited for daily living and use at home or in the residential setting, might not be best suited for the classroom or general social environments. For this reason it might serve the child's best interest to develop symbols, vocabularies, and aids to fit given environments. One family found it necessary to keep a symbol display and vocabulary board in the glove compartment of the car in order to carry on effective communication with their child while traveling. On the other hand, that same vocabulary display was not appropriate or useful at home or in school, and other symbols and vocabularies were selected and developed accordingly.

Some children who are not physically handicapped may be greatly restricted by the use of physical displays such as communication boards and books. For these individuals, it may be well to investigate the use of manual signing, or total communication, a communication system frequently used with hearing impaired and deaf individuals. Since the basic discussion of such systems as they relate to the hearing impaired is treated by Maestas y Moores and Moores in this volume, little time will be spent on the topic. However, it is important to point out that manual signing and total communication systems have been used effectively as augmentative systems with many severely cognitively and emotionally handicapped children (Schaeffer, 1979). It is important to note that if a manual or total communication system is selected for a child, the individual must have attained a cognitive functioning level of sensorimotor stage V or VI. One cannot expect a child to use Finger Spelling as a communication means until the child reaches the developmental level of approximately age seven. The specific signing system which is best suited to a given child may be a personal decision or one governed by what the largest community of users within the family's community environment might be. On the other hand, the author has a preference for using Signing Exact English (SEE) for those children who have serious developmental delays because there is a one-to-one correspondence between the sign being expressed and the spoken word that accompanies it. Learning a communication system will be difficult for many multiply handicapped children, and our responsibility is to assist in making the task simple, yet providing the most effective system possible.

Some advantages of the total communication system are its portability, its expediency, and in many cases, its less strenuous cognitive demands. Certainly the disadvantages of using the total communication system are that it has a limited audience and interactive availability. Unless there are a number of persons in the community who use sign language, the child may be using a communicatively restricted system. Other limitations are related to the need for good motor control. Communicating in sign language rules out using the hands for most ordinary purposes while signing, and the audience must be watching the message sender in order to receive the message. With respect to this latter point, it is also a problem with users of nonautomated communication boards, where a receiver must be present and attentive to the communication board during the communication interaction.

There are a variety of symbol systems available which have been adapted to communication board use. These systems have been discussed in more detail by Vanderheiden and Harris-Vanderheiden (1976), Harris and Vanderheiden (1979), Clark and Woodcock (1976), and Kates, McNaughton, and Silvermann (1977). The professional team should keep the following considerations in mind when selecting the symbol system to be used with a given aid or technique:

1. Is the symbol system and vocabulary compatible with the aid or technique selected?
2. Does it allow for the greatest interaction with the fewest number of symbols? (Space becomes a premium.)
3. Is the system and the vocabulary selected appropriate for the child's cognitive level, language comprehension skills, motor competency and environmental demands?
4. Is the system dynamic, developmentally based, generative and flexible to allow for the child's future growth and changes?
5. Is the system acceptable to the child, parents, caregivers, teachers and those persons with whom the individual will interact most fre-

quently? The most commonly used ones are: photos, pictures and/ or line drawings, Blissymbols, and traditional orthography (words, for example).

For young children and low-functioning children, pictures and photos may be the most appropriate elements. The child using a picture vocabulary system usually points to pictures that represents objects, ideas, or thoughts. For the young child who has been pointing to objects for communicative purposes, an appropriate transition is to have photos made of the objects the child has been using for interaction, and have those mounted on a display for communication use. Subsequently, pictures from magazines or black and white line drawings may be substituted for the photos. The size of the pictures selected will, or course, depend upon the child's visual, motor, and perceptual skills. Size of pictures may also be determined by the number of picture symbols which need to be placed on the communication board display. Pictures are applicable to nearly all of the basic techniques and aids, except for the higher-level independent aids that have some form of printout display. In any case, pictures are usually thought of as the easiest system to implement with young children and mentally retarded children. On the other hand, adolescent mentally retarded persons may become resentful when pictures are routinely used, because they feel they are being treated as "babies."

In the last several years, Blissymbolics have become popular and useful for many nonspeaking persons, both with normal and delayed cognitive functioning (Harris and others, 1975; Harris and others, 1979; Kates, McNaughton and Silvermann, 1977). Blissymbolics are ideographic symbols that represent concepts (as opposed to words only) through simple line drawings. These symbols are both pictographic and ideographic, which means that they are both "picture-like" and representative of an idea or concept. Like picture systems, Blissymbolics can be used with young prereading and cognitively low-functioning individuals (Harris and others, 1979). Because symbolics are idea-based rather than object-based, as picture systems are, they are able to evoke generalizations more effectively than pictures. They also contain many concepts and abstractions that could not be easily depicted with pictures, such as affective responses of "hurt", "happy," and so forth.

Blissymbolics, like pictures, may be applicable to and used on all of the basic techniques and aids. Even some independent aids have a printout for symbolics. The symbolic may serve as a transitional system for the child who is not yet ready for traditional orthography, but is in need of a more versatile system than pictures offer. Because of the linguistic nature of the Blissymbolic, it has been found to facilitate the acquistion of language, and has enhanced communication initiation and interactive skills (Harris and others, 1979).

Traditional Orthography (T.O.) has been used on communication cards for years. Basically, T.O. is the twenty-six-letter alphabet system, and all words in the T.O. system are formed by combining these letters. The twenty-six letters can be placed on the communication aid, allowing the child an unlimited vocabulary potential. This, of course, assumes that the child is at a developmental level where spelling is an option. On the other hand, it is possible to place words on the communication aid. This requires that the child be able to read. Also, there is some limitation to the number of words which can ultimately be placed on the communication board; therefore, the size of the printed word should accommodate both visual and motor ability.

Because T.O. is the system used by nonhandicapped persons, it is often preferred by parents and teachers who want the child to appear and be as "unhandicapped" as possible. If T.O. is to be used, one must keep in mind that the child will be required to learn to read and spell before he or she can communicate effectively. It is well to keep in mind that the nonhandicapped child is not asked to acquire reading and spelling skills until long after he or she has mastered the skill of speech communication. T.O. is a skill which should certainly be learned by all children who are cognitively able to do so.

The T.O. system can be applied to aids and techniques at all levels of implementation. It is the most versatile of the systems, but the entry level for effective use is about seven years developmentally (Clark and Woodcock, 1976).

Introducing the Child to an Augmentative Symbol System

Just as spoken words are natural symbol models for children who will develop speech, and children develop familiarity with them prior to using speech, the symbols which the nonspeech child will use should become familiar to him or her prior to their communicative use. The augmentative symbol system which the child will be using for communicative purposes (pictures, Blissymbolics, orthography) should be visually available to the child before they are taught or used in communication. The symbols should always be used in conjunction with speech in interacting with the child, and in interacting with other persons in the child's presence. Pairing the symbols with spoken words/objects and persons in the environment should assist the child in learning their referential status and meaning.

Factors to Consider When Comparing Augmentative Communication Aids and Systems

The job of selecting the most appropriate augmentative communication aid and symbol system for the child is complex, and at times almost forbidding. The system, however, must be continually under observation and scrutiny. There are various factors which must be under constant and consistent consideration by the team, some of which are:

1. The *speed* with which the child can communicate with others. Most persons are impatient listeners at best, and if the child's system is a slow one, the message receiver may spend little time interacting.

2. The *degree of independence* which the system allows. Is it possible to put together the message intended to be sent, and then call the person's attention to the fact that the sender has something to "say"? It is also important for the system to allow for initiating communication, as well as being one which has basic respondent characteristics.

3. The *availability* of the augmentative aid or the materials for its construction. If there is a six-month wait for an aid, or it takes a highly skilled engineer to make an aid in a community where one is not available, valuable time and effort may be lost. Various aid options should be investigated to find what might be a best fit, and also readily available. Another consideration is the availability of service to repair aids. Even the best aids will need repairs. Physically handicapped persons are not as well coordinated as nonhandicapped persons, and the probability of dropping aids is high. Many aids are relatively fragile and "down time" for an aid may be of considerable consequence to the user.

4. The *cost* of an aid and system. Aids can vary in cost from a few dollars, for those homemade boards of plywood, to thousands of dollars for independent electronic varieties. One must consider carefully what will be accomplished by the more expensive aid that cannot be taken care of by a less expensive aid. An electronic scanning aid with a limited display may be cheaper than one with a larger display, but will the child have outgrown the smaller display aid in six months and need the larger one? Who pays for a communication aid becomes of concern for many persons. To date, some private insurance companies pay for "communication prostheses," but for the most part, aids must be paid for by the family or community service agencies. At no time should the cost of an aid be the sole determinant for recommending one aid over another, but it must be given serious consideration when there are cheaper but comparable options are available.

5. The *acceptance* of the aid or system *by the child,* the family, and the educational system. Best laid plans and recommendations may be of little value if the system selected is not acceptable to the user as well as those with whom the child will communicate. Whenever possible, it might be wise to allow a child to have experience with more than one type of communication aid or symbol system. There are frequent debates as to whether the child should be taught to use a signing system or a communication aid with a symbol system. Such considerations must be given careful thought, but a good principle to keep in mind is: Which system will allow the child to have the most interaction socially, educationally and, eventually, vocationally?

6. The *practicality* of the system. Is the system and aid we have selected for the user so complex that most message receivers react negatively to it? Communication is for interaction purposes. If the system selected discourages interaction with others, including peers, then we have not selected the appropriate aid and system. In many cases we are finding that children who have become interactive with peers, using a Blissymbolics system, move on to traditional orthography for reading purposes. This is to be encouraged; however, if

all the peers are using Blissymbolics, it is best to have the child use the Blissymbolics board for peer interaction. When the peers are also using traditional orthography, a complete switch may be made, thus allowing the child to use the system which best fits the social community.

7. The *allowance for flexibility*. Much time can be spent in making aids and displays. There should be room on the board for adding symbols, and materials should be used so that symbols can be moved about on the board. One important advantage of Blissymbolics and traditional orthography is an infinite number of vocabulary possibilities; the basic limitation is the space on the display itself. From that standpoint, we need to provide a vocabulary that has the most potential use possible.

Conclusion

Communication development for the nonspeaking child, as with all individuals, is an ongoing process. Continued evaluation is needed to assist nonspeaking individuals in expanding their communication systems to meet changing needs.

There is wide variation in the communication needs and abilities of individuals who can use augmentative systems. For some children, particularly those who are physically handicapped, it can be the difference between participating in the activities around them, or simply watching others act. For many multiply handicapped persons, an effective communication aid will have important effects on the personal, social, and educational process, as well as future vocation considerations. For others, an appropriate communication system will permit them to systematically communicate their needs, and to express emotions in a manner understandable to others.

References

Bruner, J. S. "From Communication to Language: A Psychological Perspective." *Cognition*, 1975, *3*, 255–287.

Chapman, R. S., and Miller, J. F. "Analyzing Language and Communication in the Child." In R. L. Schiefelbusch, (Ed.), *Nonspeech Language Intervention*. Baltimore: University Park Press, 1979.

Clark, C., and Woodcock, R. "Graphic Systems of Communication." In L. Lloyd, (Ed.), *Communication Assessment and Intervention Strategies*, Baltimore: University Park Press, 1976.

Harris, D., Brown, W. P., McKenzie, P., Riener, S., and Scheibel, C. "Symbol Communication for the Mentally Handicapped." *Mental Retardation*, 1975, *13* (1).

Harris, D., Lippert, J., Yoder, D., and Vanderheiden, G. "Blissymbols: An Augmentative Symbol Communication System for Nonvocal Severely Handicapped Children." In R. York, and E. Edgar, (Eds.), *Teaching the Severely Handicapped*. Vol 4. Columbus, Ohio: Special Press, 1979.

Harris, D., and Vanderheiden, G. "Enhancing Communicative Interaction Skills in Nonvocal Severely Physically Handicapped Children." In R. L. Schiefelbusch, (Ed.), *Nonspeech Language Intervention*. Baltimore: University Park Press, 1979.

Kates, B., McNaughton, S., and Silvermann, H. *Handbook for Instructors, Users, Parents, and Administraters.* Toronto, Ontario: Blissymbolic Communication Foundation, 1977.

Piaget, J. *The Origins of Intelligence in Children.* New York: Norton, 1964.

Reichle, J. E., and Yoder, D. E. "Communicative Behavior for the Severely and Profoundly Mentally Retarded: Assessment and Early Stimulation Strategies." In R. York and G. Edgar (Eds.), *Teaching the Severely Handicapped,* Vol. 4. Columbus, Ohio: Special Press, 1979.

Schaeffer, B. "Spontaneous Language Through Signed Speech." In R. L. Schiefelbusch (Ed.), *Nonspeech Language Intervention,* Baltimore: University Park Press, 1979.

Vanderheiden, G., and Grilley, K. *Nonvocal Communication Techniques and Aids for the Severely Physically Handicapped.* Baltimore: University Park Press, 1975.

Vanderheiden, G. and Grilley, K. *Nonvocal Communication Techniques and Aids for the Severely Physically Handicapped.* Baltimore: University Park Press, 1975.

Vanderheiden, G., and Harris-Vanderheiden, D. "Communication Techniques and Aids for the Nonvocal Severely Physically Handicapped." In L. Lloyd (Ed.), *Communication Assessment and Intervention Strategies.* Baltimore: University Park Press, 1976.

Vicker, B. *Non-Oral Communication System Project.* Ames: University Stores, University of Iowa, 1974.

Yarrow, L., Klein, R., Lomonaco, S., and Morgan, G. "Cognitive and Motivational Development in Early Childhood." In B. Friedlander, G. Sterritt, and G. Kirk (Eds.), *Exceptional Infant.* Vol. 3. New York: Brunner-Mazel, 1975.

David Yoder is a professor of communicative disorders and head of Communication Aids and Systems Clinic at the University of Wisconsin, Madison.

*Children from low-income backgrounds often need assistance in
developing facility with the language of school instruction.
An effective system for improving language in this population
is described.*

Direct Instruction Language

Jean Osborn
Wesley C. Becker

Most educators agree that kindergarten children who are facile with spoken language and who demonstrate an understanding of the meanings and relationships that underlie the words they use, are children who will do well in school. Most educators also agree that children who exhibit language problems, or differences, or who seem behind in language development are children who are likely to have trouble in school. But educators do not agree that language can be taught as a formal subject in a school setting, and that if taught such language training can positively affect a child's school achievement.

In this chapter, we describe the language curriculum of a classroom model that does teach language in a highly organized and specified manner—the Oregon Direct Instruction Model. This model is one of those included in the USOE Follow Through Study, which has focused on the economically disadvantaged child. In the Follow Through Study the Direct Instruction Model was found to produce the best student progess in reading, arithmetic, and language at the end of the third grade (Becker, 1978).

We first briefly discuss the rationale from which the language program and its teaching strategies have been derived. We then discuss the program's organization, content, and how it is taught. Finally, we specify some of the instructional strategies that teachers employ as they teach language as a formal subject. Although the teachers in Direct Instruction classrooms use a published program *(DISTAR Language,* Engelmann and Osborn, 1972, 1976, 1977) as the basis for their language instruction, we believe that whether or not this specific program is used, the approach descibed here and the type of teaching associated with it will be of use to many teachers of children experiencing language problems in elementary schools.

Rationale for the Program

The Direct Instruction language curriculum is a formal program of instruction focusing on the language of schools. It includes the important elements of instructional language as well as some of the broader knowledge of the words and sentence structures relevant to reading comprehension. A major premise of this model is that children attending school must understand the language used for instruction in classrooms, as well as the language that appears in texts and workbooks. The directions and teaching demonstrations used by teachers for the teaching of arithmetic, reading, social studies, science, and other school subjects are classified as instructional language. The language used by teachers to direct the sequence of events during a school day — as well as the directions and instructional sequences that appear in textbooks and workbooks — are other instances of instructional language. The language of textbooks and workbooks also includes a broad range of world knowledge, the vocabulary associated with it, and a wide variety of sentence structures. An understanding of the concepts represented by this vocabulary and these sentence structures is crucial to reading comprehension.

It is our conviction that instructional language can be systematically taught by limiting the scope of what is to be presented, by organizing the content into teachable tasks, and by carefully sequencing the tasks into a daily program. While the language of feelings and social interaction is not a focus of the Direct Instruction language program, we believe that a school program should also include activities which foster the use of such language. Language has many facets, but only some of those facets can be efficiently taught through teacher-directed instruction.

Organization of the Program

Clarity of concept presentations and provisions for the cumulative use and application of what is taught are the primary programming goals of our language curriculum. To achieve these goals, lesson scripts are provided to indicate what the teacher does and says, and what the children are to do and say. Lessons are comprised of tasks. Tasks are constructed as elements of sequences in which related sets of concepts are presented. Examples of sequences are: prepositions, identity statements, polars, if-then reasoning. Sequences run for ten to forty days. There are about eight to ten tasks in a lesson; students work on several sequences during one lesson. Within sequences, tasks progress from those in which there is much teacher demonstration to those in which the students respond to minimal teacher cues.

What is taught in one sequence is frequently used as a component of a more advanced sequence. For example, in the first level of the program, the students are taught opposites (big-little, tall-short) as a part of the polars sequence. They are taught what objects are made of (paper, wood) as a part of the materials sequence. They are also taught class terms (animal, vehicle, container) in the classification sequence. What the children know from each of these sequences is utilized in the analogy sequence in the second level of the program. Among the analogies the students construct are: (1) "A mouse is to short as giraffe is to tall", (2) "A truck is to big as car is to little", and (3) "A bag is to paper as a box is to wood." The children also learn to tell what analogies are about; for the above analogies they determine that the first one is about "an animal to its size," the second is about "a vehicle is to its size," and the third is about "a container is to what is made of."

The practice of utilizing, in advanced sequences, information that has been taught in previous sequences serves two functions (1) It enables students to learn new, more complex concepts more quickly. If students know the basic concepts (animal-size, vehicle-size, container-material) used to illustrate more advanced concepts (analogical reasoning and underlying rules), they can concentrate on the new operations involved in the advanced concepts; (2) It permits students to constantly practice using and generalizing basic language concepts to a broad number of situations.

Content of the Program

Level One includes sequences in identity and action statements, prepositions, singular and plural statements, pronouns, verb tense, polars, comparatives, and-or, classification, part-whole relationships, some-all-none, same-different, before-after, if-then, who-where-when-what, as well as basic information such as days of the week, months and seasons of the year, colors, shapes, the names and definitions of different occupations, locations, and some natural phenomena.

Level Two devotes considerable time to tasks and word analysis skills, such as: definitions, descriptions, absurdities, analogies, if-then, true-false, questioning skills, statement analysis, synonyms, superlatives, and contractions. More general information is also presented, such as materials, part-whole objects, land forms (islands, peninsulas, continents) and some directional skills such as left-right, from-to, and map reading.

The application of the concepts and statements taught in both levels occurs in the problem-solving tasks and logical games that appear in almost every lesson.

The major focus of Level Three is on the analysis of sentences, both spoken and written. The emphasis is on analysis that deals with what a sentence says and what inferences can be logically drawn from that sentence. In the sequence of task activities, this kind of analysis is systematically extended to writing. The students spend a good part of almost every lesson writing sentences and then paragraphs. They also learn punctuation and capitalization rules and do some grammatical analysis as well. There are also sequences in which analogies and formal deductions are presented. By the end of the program students can identify subjects and predicates, can transform sentences from one verb tense to another and can identify statements, questions, and commands.

How the Program Is Taught

The program is designed so that students take part in demonstrations of basic concepts and then practice making statements in which those concepts are imbedded. As the students progress through the three levels of the program, lessons change from those in which almost all of the lesson time is spent in oral interaction between the children and the teacher to those in which the students spend most of the lesson time doing independent written work. Children at the beginning levels (kindergarten or first grade) spend about thirty minutes a day in language instruction; second and third grade children are engaged for about forty minutes in a combination of teacher-directed oral work and independently done written work. In the first and second levels of the program, the teacher works with groups ranging in size from five to fifteen children. In the third level the teacher usually works with the entire class. Some children can finish the three levels in two years; others, who have more to learn, may take four years. Most children in the Direct Instruction classrooms take three years to complete the program (Becker and Engelmann, 1978).

The language program should be as definite a part of the school day as is instruction in arithmetic, science, and social studies. The instruction maximizes student participation and practice. During the lesson the teacher presents instructions and asks questions; the students respond orally, usually as a group. The students also respond by performing actions and by pointing to objects or pictures. The student responses provide instant and accurate feedback to the teacher about what is being learned from the teacher presentation. All mistakes and ambiguous responses are corrected in a matter-of-fact and positive manner. The children's responses dictate the rate at which the teacher can procede through the lesson. The number of student-teacher interchanges varies from lesson to lesson and from level to level, but is is not unusual (in the first two levels of the program) for 200 student utterances to occur during a half-hour instructional period. This amount of practice is made possible because of several instructional strategies:

1. Tasks are designed so that student responses are elicited as a part of the presentation. For example, the teacher says, "Everyone, *show me* the elephant that is big," and not "*Look at* the elephant that is big."

2. Children respond together, which means that each child in the group gets much more practice than if the only responses are individual responses. For example, the teacher says, "Tell me about what this elephant is doing." ("Sleeping.") "Now, everybody, let's all say the whole thing about what the elephant is doing." ("This elephant is sleeping.") Instead of "Who can tell what the elephant is doing? Mary, you tell us." ("Sleeping.")

The teacher does call on individual children, but only after the teacher feels the group has had sufficient practice.

3. The language lesson proceeds at a fast pace. The statement-repetition task (actions) in Figure 1 usually takes less than two minutes of lesson time, if the students have mastered all of the components of the task that were presented in earlier lessons.

4. Students must use the language concepts they are learning in problem solving tasks.

The first page of a concept application task from the level one language program is shown in Figure 2. The concepts the children must use to solve the problem, "Which apple will the rabbit eat?" are future tense, actions, polar relationships (big-little) and part-whole relationships (leaves-apple), as well as the process of combining two descriptive attributes. All of these concepts have been presented in the lessons preceding this one. Application tasks appear in almost every lesson starting at lesson forty-four of the first level program.

The statement-repetition and the statement-application tasks in the program are important. In order to comprehend what they read, children must be able to process words in written statements. It is our observation that many children with reading comprehension difficulties also have difficulty accurately repeating spoken statements. One of the goals of the language program is to give the children enough practice saying and using a variety of statement forms so that they are in a better position to understand them when they read them. Statement repetition and practice tasks should always be associated with *meaning*. The children practice using statements to describe what they are looking at, are doing, or thinking about. The statements the children use get longer as they progress through the program.

Some Important Strategies for Effective Teaching

1. Before beginning this program, children need to have in their repertoire the following basic language behaviors:

      a. The ability to imitate a word or phrase spoken by an adult; for example, "A dog" or "On the table."

Figure 1.

LESSON 55

TASK 1 Actions

It's time for some actions.
a. Everybody, touch your hips. Signal.
   Wait. What are you doing? Signal.
   Touching my hips.
b. Everybody, hold your hand on your shoulder.
   Signal. Wait. What are you doing? Signal.
   Holding my hand on my shoulder.
c. Everybody, hold your hand over
   your shoulder. Signal. Wait.
   What are you doing? Signal.
   Holding my hand over my shoulder.
d. Everybody, hold your hand in front
   of your neck. Signal. Wait.
   What are you doing? Signal.
   Holding my hand in front of my neck.
e. Everybody, hold your hand in front
   of your eye. Signal. Wait.
   What are you doing? Signal.
   Holding my hand in front of my eye.
f. Repeat a through e until all children's
   responses are firm.

g. Everybody, hold your hand over
   your shoulder. Signal. Wait.
   What are you doing? Signal.
   Holding my hand over my shoulder.
   Say the whole thing. Signal.
   I am holding my hand over my shoulder.
h. Everybody, hold your hand on your shoulder.
   Signal. Wait. What are you doing? Signal.
   Holding my hand on my shoulder.
   Say the whole thing. Signal.
   I am holding my hand on my shoulder.
i. Everybody, hold your hand in front of your
   neck. Signal. Wait. What are you doing?
   Signal. *Holding my hand in front of
   my neck.* Say the whole thing. Signal.
   I am holding my hand in front of my neck.

j. Everybody, touch your hips. Signal. Wait.
   What are you doing? Signal.
   Touching my hips. Say the whole thing.
   Signal. *I am touching my hips.*
k. Everybody, hold your hand in front of your
   eye. Signal. Wait. What are you doing?
   Signal. *Holding my hand in front of my eye.*
   Say the whole thing. Signal.
   I am holding my hand in front of my eye.
l. Repeat g through k until all children's
   responses are firm.

m. Everybody, hold your hand on your shoulder.
   Signal. Wait. What are you doing? Signal.
   Holding my hand on my shoulder.
   Are you holding your hand over your
   shoulder? Signal. *No.*
   Say the whole thing. Signal.
   I am not holding my hand over my shoulder.
n. What are you doing? Signal.
   Holding my hand on my shoulder.
   Say the whole thing. Signal.
   I am holding my hand on my shoulder.

Individual Test
Repeat a through n, calling on different
children for each step.

---

b. The ability to answer questions in the form of "What is this?" or
   "What are you doing?" (or to learn this quickly).
c. The ability to answer simple yes/no questions; for example,
   "Are you sitting?", "Is this a dog?"
d. The ability to point to and label common objects; for example,
   "A chair," "A pencil," and simple actions, for example,
   "Standing," or "Smiling."
e. The ability to understand that objects and actions can be
   described using the same words that are used to name actual
   objects and actions.

These are the minimum requirements for entry into the program. The
list is not exhaustive; most of the children we work with exhibit a much greater

Figure 2.

TASK 5 Concept Application

Look at the picture.
The rabbit will eat only one of these apples.

a. Listen. The rabbit will eat the big apple that has leaves. Which apple will it eat? Signal. Respond with the children. *The big apple that has leaves.*

b. Say the whole thing about the apple the rabbit will eat. Signal. *The rabbit will eat the big apple that has leaves.*

c. Point to 1.
Is this apple big? Touch. *Yes.*
Does this apple have leaves? Touch. *No.*
So will the rabbit eat this apple? Touch. *No.*

d. Why won't the rabbit eat this apple? Touch. *It doesn't have leaves.*

e. Repeat c and d until all children's responses are firm.

f. Point to 2.
Is this apple big? Touch. *Yes.*
Does this apple have leaves? Touch. *Yes.*
So will the rabbit eat this apple? Touch. *Yes.*

g. How do you know the rabbit will eat this apple? Touch. *It's big and it has leaves.*

h. Repeat f and g until all children's responses are firm.

i. Point to 3.
Is this apple big? Touch. *No.*
Does this apple have leaves? Touch. *Yes.*
So will the rabbit eat this apple? Touch. *No.*

j. Why won't the rabbit eat this apple? Touch. *It isn't big.*
Repeat i and j until all children's responses are firm.

k. Point to 4.
Is this apple big? Touch. *No.*
Does this apple have leaves? Touch. *No.*
So will the rabbit eat this apple? Touch. *No.*

l. Why won't the rabbit eat this apple? Touch. *It isn't big and it doesn't have leaves.*
Repeat k and l until all children's responses are firm.

m. Say the whole thing about the apple the rabbit will eat. Signal. *The rabbit will eat the big apple that has leaves.*
Let's see if you are right.
Turn the page quickly.

range of language skills than those described above. Children whose language does not include these behaviors have to be taught them before they attempt the program. Children whose first language is not English, but who have acquired these behaviors in their native language can begin instruction in English at the first level of the program.

2. Those children who require the most language instruction are those children who are frequently the most difficult to teach. It is important to have such children in small groups (no more than seven) so that the teacher can hear student responses more accurately and can engage the children in the often intense practice necessary to achieve statement-making facility. For these children, the process of pairing and chaining the steps in logical reasoning tasks is especially important. Small groups permit the teacher to check on each child as the teacher procedes through the chain of steps. These students should also have a maximum amount of instructional time made available to them.

3. Children should be able to correctly respond to all of the steps in a task before the teacher leaves the task. This teaching strategy is especially important when working with hard-to-teach children, and it is critical in those tasks which involve logical reasoning. It took one of the authors of this paper about five minutes to teach the following task (which is in the middle of the classification sequence) to a group of six-year-old, hard-to-teach children. Different children in the group made errors at almost every step in the task. The teaching procedure that was used is shown in Figure 3. Each mistake the teacher heard was corrected instantly (either by the teacher or by another student). The question which prompted the mistake was repeated and the correct answer was given by the group. Then the teacher went back to the beginning of the task and presented each segment again; the students responded. When another error occurred, the teacher corrected, repeated the segment and returened to the beginning of the task. At the end of the five-minute period, the teacher (to check her impression that the students understood the task) presented two parallel tasks which the students went through without error.

4. What the teacher does during the rest of the school day to use the language of the lesson in other situations affects how the students generalize and transfer what they are being taught. The more difficult a child is to teach and the more he has to be taught, the greater is the need for the teacher to provide for activities that transfer what is taught in the language lesson to the remainder of the classroom day and to the playground. We have observed that teachers become very conscious of the language used in the lessons. In every day classroom activities they come to "naturally" emphasize prepositional relationships, singular-plural discriminations, same-different comparisons, and so forth, as these occur in the language program.

5. A danger of group responses is that the responses are permitted to become loud and stilted. If group responses are too loud, the teacher cannot hear individual children's errors; if the group responses sounds stilted, the children are

Figure 3.

20

TASK 3 Classification

We're going to talk about classes.

a. If we took all cups from the class of
containers, would there be any kinds of
containers left? Signal. *Yes.*

b. Name some kinds of containers that would
be left. Call on different children.
Praise appropriate responses.

c. The class of cups is made up of many
kinds of cups. I'll name some kinds of
cups in the class of cups. Listen. Blue
cups, red cups, yellow cups.
You name some kinds of cups in the class
of cups. Call on different children.
Praise reasonable answers, such as blue
cups, white cups, red cups.

d. Think about this. If we took all the
yellow cups from the class of cups, would
there be any cups left? Signal. *Yes.*

e. Name some kinds of cups that would be
left. Call on different children.
Praise all acceptable answers: that is,
any kind of cup except yellow cups.

f. Yes, if we took all the yellow cups from
the class of cups, there would still be
cups left.
So which class is bigger, the class of
cups or the class of yellow cups?
Signal. *The class of cups.*
How do you know? Signal. *The class of
cups has more kinds of things in it.*

g. Think big. Which class is bigger, the
class of containers or the class of cups?
Signal. *The class of containers.*

h. Think big. Which class is bigger, the
class of yellow cups or the class of cups?
Signal. *The class of cups.*

Individual Test
Repeat *g* and *h,* calling on different children.

not practicing natural language. Teachers must not permit their students to fall into either of these response modes.

Teaching from a Script

Contrary to what might be expected, good teachers find teaching from a script very satisfactory. Teachers have commented that having a script to follow permits them to concentrate on what the students are saying and to respond to what they are doing. Figure 4 is an attempt to record the strategies a teacher is employing as she teaches analogies from the second level of the program to a group of eight children. The script that Miss Harris is working from is shown in Figure 4 (what Miss Harris is thinking is enclosed in parenthesis).

"All right children, here's the first task. Listen, we're going to do some more *analogies*. You're going to figure out what an *analogy* is about." (We've spent about three or four minutes of every half-hour language lesson during the past nineteen lessons on analogies. Those tasks began so simply, but every day they got a little harder, something more was added. And just yesterday, we began a format which sets up the kids for figuring out the *rule* that underlies an analogy they have worked on. Processing these analogies requires a kind of abstract thinking that I would have said these kids could not possibly manage. But they are *good* at it.)

Miss Harris raised her hand and said, "Listen to this: A bottle is to glass as a bag is to . . ." and paused about two seconds. (It's better that they know they have time to really figure out the answer than to think they are going to have to say it fast. If you signal this kind of response too quickly, you cause the kids to start guessing and to give foolish answers.) She dropped her hand, six children said "Paper," and two children said, "Plastic." Miss Harris said, "Paper, plastic. Right. Let's use paper." Then she repeated the step.

She then asked, "What class are a bottle and a glass in?" (There will be no problems here. They've been doing classification since last year.) She lowered her hand and everyone said, "Containers." "Yes," said Miss Harris, "Containers. Our analogy tells about containers." (I'm telling them they are right *and* repeating their correct answer. That is the *confirming response*.)

Miss Harris repeated the analogy. "A bottle is to glass as a bag is to paper." (Here we go into these questions. They've had analogies that come from all of these rules, but we haven't talked about all the rules yet. They had trouble with a couple of them yesterday, but I think they've got it today.) She asked the first question, "Does our analogy tell what you put in those containers?" (I am watching Tom and Maria, my two most difficult children; they are watching me. Here I go.) She signaled the response. Tom and Maria said, "No." (I'm sure about them, and I didn't hear anything but "no" from the rest. Let's go to the next question—fast.) She then said, "Does our analogy tell what parts they have?" The group said, "No." (They're doing fine. I can even hear

Figure 4.

TASK 2 Analogies

You're going to figure out what an analogy is about.

a. Listen to this: A bottle is to glass as a bag is to . . . (signal) *paper.*

b. What class are a bottle and a bag in? Signal. *Containers.* Yes, containers. Our analogy tells something about containers.

c. A bottle is to glass as a bag is to paper. Does our analogy tell what you put in the containers? Signal. *No.*
Does our analogy tell what they are made of? Signal. *Yes.*
Does our analogy tell what parts they have? Signal. *No.*
Does our analogy tell what class they are in? Signal. *No.*
So our analogy tells what they are made of. Repeat c until responses are firm.

d. What is a bottle made of? Signal. *Glass.* Say the first part of the analogy.
Signal. *A bottle is to glass.*

e. What is a bag made of? Signal. *Paper.* Say the next part of the analogy. Signal. *A bag is to paper.*

f. What does the analogy tell us about the containers? Signal. *What they are made of.* Yes, what they are made of.

g. Everybody, say the whole analogy. Signal. *A bottle is to glass as a bag is to paper.*

h. Repeat f and g until all responses are firm.

Susan. Let's move on.) "Does our analogy tell what those containers are made of?" She signaled the response, and everyone said, "Yes," except for Linda who said a big, loud "No." (Oh, here we go, Linda may get upset over this one. She was really wrong, all the others said, "Yes." Now she knows that she was wrong and she knows that the others know she gave the wrong answer. Instead, I'm going to give her another chance to go through this task.) Miss Harris said, "Listen, everyone: A bottle is to glass as a bag is to paper. A bottle is made of . . . " "Paper," said the children. "So," said Miss Harris, "Think about it, does that analogy tell what those containers are *made* of?" She signaled and all the children said, "Yes." (Hurrah. Linda answered correctly. Correcting everyone at once even though only one child made the mistake is much better.

You never know who is going to make the same kind of mistake on the next trial. It's a lot better to give everyone the practice than to have one child do it alone. It also keeps everyone amused. And Linda didn't feel picked on.)

Then Miss Harris asked the question, "Does our analogy tell where you find them?" She signaled and everyone said, "No." (Now we'll run those yes-no questions once more, really fast. In fact, I'll challenge these kids a little.) "Okay kids, let's see if you can answer all of these questions without any mistakes. If you do, I'll think you're smart." Miss Harris asked each of the questions again, she spoke very quickly, emphasizing the words in each sentence that were particularly important for the children to listen to. She paused about two seconds before signaling each response. She moved the "yes" question to the second place, so that no one could get the answer by remembering the order of the questions. She looked straight at Linda during the question she had missed. She was careful not to mouth the answers herself as the children answered the questions. There were no mistakes. Then she said, "Right. And I *do* think you are smart!"

She asked, "What is a bottle made of?" She signaled and the children said, "Glass." Then she said, "Say the first part of the analogy." The children said. "A bottle is to glass." Then she said, "What is a bag made of?" and signaled the response. Then she said, "Say the second part of the analogy." The children said, "A bottle is to glass." Then she said, "What is a bag made of?" and signaled the response. Then she said, "Say the second part of the analogy." The children said, "A bag is to paper." (So far so good. They got that without any repetition or correcting. Look at that Tom, he is on the edge of his chair. And look at Jonah and Juan at the ends of the row. They haven't taken their eyes off me since we started this. Such rapt attention does contribute to teacher satisfaction. But now comes the hard part.)

She said, "This is the hard part. What does the analogy *tell* us about the containers?" Her eyes swept around the group, and she watched each child say, "What they are made of." (We did it. They did it. But I'm going to save the praise until I'm sure they can discriminate the analogy from this rule they've just figured out.) She finished the task, first asking the children to say the analogy, then asking what the analogy tells about the containers, and finally having them say the analogy again. There were no mistakes. She gave Kent and Linda and Marie individual turns on the discrimination steps and then said, "You are smart children today. This is hard stuff and you are learning this fast." (And they are. But where would we be today if we hadn't done that last step about fifteen times yesterday? Even then, I didn't think Tom and Susan were really sure about the difference in the two statements when we left yesterday. But I should have been more optimistic, and today I am—at least until tomorrow.)

This task took Miss Harris about three minutes to teach. Yesterday a similar task took five minutes, but the time she spent "correcting and firming" had really paid off today. (By tomorrow we'll really be able to zip through this task. Teaching it yesterday with all that repeating was not particularly fun. I bet we did that task ten times and that's not counting repeating separate steps within the task. And I did check out *everyone* on an individual turn.) As Miss Harris moved on to the next task, she knew she had taught the analogy task so that each child could do it without any prompting and without any correction. She also knew that each child could perform well on parallel tasks. She also knew she would be able to begin tomorrow's analogies task with the confidence that each of the children had the skills prerequisite to cope with the task.

She realized that the skills prerequisite to today's task took a long time to teach. In fact, she began teaching them the first day of school in the first language lesson she taught the group.

The Need for Language Instruction in Schools

Children who come from homes where there is strong adult support for refining the use of language are more likely to succeed in school than those from homes with less adult-child contact and adults with less education. This conclusion is shared by many educational researchers (Coleman, 1975; Freeberg and Payne, 1967; Glass, 1973; Bereiter and Engelmann, 1966; Becker, 1977). The position offered in this paper is that children from homes where there is strong adult support for refining the use of language will continue to be the *only* group of children to reliably experience school success unless there is a concerted and wide-ranging effort made to develop intensive and systematic language programs as a central part of the curriculum of elementary and secondary schools.

Since 1967 the project we have worked with has served some 30,000 low-income students in schools in twenty different school districts in the United States. This experience has convinced us that most school programs are designed to accommodate middle-class students. We believe this to be the case even in those schools which primarily serve children from poor and under educated familites. In order for schools to be capable of serving all students, it is our conviction that school programs need to be redesigned. Central to such a redesign is a systematic language curriculum (kindergarten through high school) capable of providing effective instruction in vocabulary, statement making, question asking and logical reasoning strategies. Such a language program would have to be far more extensive and involve many more direct specific instructional practices than is typical of current language arts curricula.

Becker (1977) has suggested some language analysis strategies that might be used to define an average adult vocabulary. Once identified, this vocabulary could be analyzed for its common form structures (what Dixon and Engelmann [1979] have termed morphographs) and its "core" meaning structure. The analysis would provide a basis for more systematic construction of textbooks in all content areas to facilitate growth of language through the careful building on a known base. Some of the analytic studies now in progress at the University of Oregon may, before long, provide the basis of a new generation of curricula that include coordinated language instruction as an essential element.

References

Becker, W. C. "Teaching Reading and Language to the Disadvantaged—What We Have Learned from Field Research." *Harvard Educational Review,* 1977, *47* (4), 518–543.

Becker, W. C. "The National Evaluation of Follow Through—Behavior-Theory-Based Programs Come Out on Top." *Education and Urban Society,* 1978, *10* (4), 431–458.

Becker, W. C., and Engelmann, S. *Follow Through Technical Report 78-1,* Eugene: University of Oregon Follow Through Project, 1978.

Bereiter, C., and Engelmann, S. *Teaching Disadvantaged Children in the Preschool.* Englewood Cliffs, N.J.: Prentice-Hall, 1966.

Coleman, J. S. "Methods and Results in the IEA Studies of Effects of School on Learning." *Review of Educational Research,* 1975, *45,* 335–386.

Dixon, R., and Englemann S. *Corrective Spelling Through Morphographics.* Chicago: Science Research Associates, 1979.

Engelmann, S., and Osborn, J. *DISTAR Language Level III.* Chicago, Science Research Associates, 1972.

Engelmann, S., and Osborn, J. *DISTAR Language Level I.* (2nd ed.) Chicago: Science Research Associates, 1976.

Engelmann, S., and Osborn, J. *DISTAR Language Level II* (2nd ed.) Chicago: Science Research Associates, 1977.

Freeberg, N. E., and Payne, W. "Parental Influence on Cognitive Development in Early Childhood: A Review." *Child Development,* 1967, *38, 65*–87.

Glass, G. W. "Problems in Implementing the Stull Act." In N. L. Gage (Ed.), *Mandated Evaluation of Education: A Conference on California's Stull Act.* Stanford, Calif: Stanford Center for Research and Development in Teaching, 1973.

Jean Osborn is a research associate at the Center for Research on Reading, University of Illinois.

Wesley Becker is a professor of education and associate dean for developmental studies at the University of Oregon.

The purpose of the volume is summarized and some general readings suggested.

Concluding Synthesis and Suggested Readings

Diane Bricker

As Schiefelbusch points out, the shifts in the conceptual basis and subsequent application of language intervention programming have been substantial. Approaching language training only as a compartmentalized set of predetermined learning activities is to miss the target of enhancing general communication functioning in the language-delayed child. The ecological model proposed by Mahoney and Weller emphasizes the need for the teacher, practitioner and parent to consider language intervention in the social context of the child's daily existence. That is, for children with emerging communication systems adequate attention must be given to establishing a preverbal, social communicative base from which a generative referential language system will develop. This theme is repeated by Bricker and Carlson who also suggest that language intervention needs to take into account the notion of developmental continuity as the young child builds from earlier, simpler behaviors to more complex response schemes. In addition, viewing the acquisition of early communicative capacities as inseparable from interrelated social, affective, motor and cognitive processes is emphasized. The teacher-clinician is advised to structure an intervention approach that reflects the multifaceted nature of communication.

The remaining three chapters in this volume provide information on intervention approaches for specific populations of communication-delayed or disordered children. The Moores highlight the empirical basis for the crucial changes that are occurring in language training with young deaf children. In particular, the point is made that substantial modifications in our approach to this severely language-handicapped group is clearly in order and in fact, past due. The Moores reflect the new and exciting "breath of life" that is being introduced in this area.

The growth in the acceptance of augmentative communication is discussed by Yoder. The sophistication of current technology provides the means for even the most severely impaired child to develop at least a basic communicative repertoire. Children who previously were forced to depend upon someone guessing or anticipating their needs are now able to exert control over their environment. The potential for augmentative systems is limited only by our lack of ingenuity in their application.

Osborn and Becker describe an intervention perspective which focuses on increasing the linguistic competence of the school-aged child who possesses a basic language repertoire but does not have the skills to understand and apply more sophisticated forms of language. The direct instruction approach has been empirically derived and demonstrated to be effective. The principles encompassed in this system may be used in conjunction with specific materials or independently to produce systematic changes in children's language.

The purpose of this volume has been to condense for the teacher, clinician and other practitioners the most current and useful information for designing and implementing language intervention programs for communicatively handicapped infants, deaf children, nonspeech children and mildly language delayed children. Economy of time for the reader required that important areas be only highlighted. For more detailed descriptions and discussions of strategies, each of the authors have provided references. In addition, a number of general readings are given below.

Suggested Readings

Bloom, L., and Lahey, M. *Language Development and Language Disorders.* New York: Wiley, 1978.

Dale, P. *Language Development.* New York: Holt, Rinehart and Winston, 1976.

deVilliers, J., and deVilliers, P. *Language Acquisition.* Cambridge, Mass.; Harvard University Press, 1978.

Guess, D., Sailor, W., and Baer, D. *Functional Speech and Language Training for the Severely Handicapped.* Lawrence, Kansas: H & H Enterprises, 1977.

Kent, L. *Language Acquisition Program for the Retarded or Multiply Impaired.* Champaign, Ill.: Research Press, 1974.

Lloyd, L., (Ed.), *Communication Assessment and Intervention Strategies.* Baltimore: University Park Press, 1976.

McLean, J., and Snyder-McLean, L. *A Transactional Approach to Early Language Training.* Columbus, Ohio: Charles Merrill, 1978.

Minifie, F., and Lloyd, L. (Eds.). *Communication and Cognitive Abilities — Early Behavioral Assessment.* Baltimore: University Park Press, 1978.

Morehead, D., and Morehead, A. (Eds.), *Normal and Deficient Child Language*. Baltimore: University Park Press, 1976.

Schiefelbusch, R. *Bases of Language Intervention*. Baltimore: University Park Press, 1979.

Diane Bricker is currently a professor of special education and director of the Preschool Program, Center on Human Development, University of Oregon. Her professional career has focused on two major areas of interest: the development of effective intervention programs for young handicapped children and the development of language programs with an emphasis on broadly based communicative functions.

Index